Tri... Thr...
A Quest for ...m and Rest

Story of Pastor Silfano Ayayo Mijema

Sam Wanyanga

Published by

_____

P.O. Box _____
_____, Kenya

© Sam Wanyanga 2017

The moral rights of the author have been asserted

All rights reserved

No part of this publication may be reproduced, distributed, or transmitted in any form or by any means, or stored in any database or retrieval system, without the prior written permission of the author and

The author assumes full responsibility for the research, quotations and all contents of this book

ISBN: 978-9966-1693-1-0

Printed by

_____

P.O. Box _____
Nairobi, Kenya

TABLE OF CONTENTS

Dedication iv
Acknowledgment v
Introduction vi
BIRTH 1
GROWING UP 13
PASTOR SILFANO'S FAMILY 23
LIGHT IN CHRISTIANITY 30
THE STRUGGLE 35
SACRILEGE 49
RESCUED BY THE SEVENTH-DAY ADVENTIST CHURCH 54
EMIGRATION 66
THE MINISTRY 73
ATTRIBUTES 85
ARRIVAL OF SEVENTH-DAY ADVENTISM IN KENYA 102
VISION 124
RETIREMENT 131

DEDICATION

This book is dedicated to all those who participated in the struggle for emancipation, which brought the Seventh-day Adventist Church to Central Kavirondo people.

ACKNOWLEDGMENT

A project of this size and magnitude takes the time and resources of many people to accomplish. It took many years in research and the valuable contribution of many people to make this book a reality. Individual contributors and a few committees provided some of the material that comprises this book. I gratefully and heartily acknowledge all those contributors.

There are several people I am indebted to whose names I must mention because of the significant role they played or contribution of materials they made toward the implementation of this project.

To Rev. Canon Francis Omondi and Amos B. Omollo who were my editorial and publishing consultants. To Emily Achieng' who spent hours typing this manuscript. To the late Pastor Tobias Otieno Ayayo, the eldest son of Pastor Silfano Ayayo Mijema, whose knowledge and recollection of the family history formed the basis and provided the seeds for writing this book.

To Martin, Edwina, Zack, Cleveland, Paul, Reina and Jim, the grandchildren of Pastor Silfano Ayayo Mijema, whose words of encouragement and analytical views fired me up.

To Juanita Trusty of U.S.A., who accorded me an enabling environment in her home where part of this book was written. To my nephew Cleveland Ayayo and niece Edwina Ombado, who contributed part of the funds that financed the expenses incurred in publishing the book. To my wife Jane (Mama Lydia) for being there for me and for ensuring that an atmosphere of peace and tranquility prevailed during the time I was writing. Most of all I give glory to God for giving me good health and for giving me His words, which formed most of the quotations in the book.

Finally I'm indeed grateful to Martin, Zach, Cleveland, Nandwa, Robinson and Reina for their splendid work in initial editing of this book, to Maxwel Onyango who helped with proof reading, and to my publisher for working with me on publishing this book.

May our all-loving God bless them.

— Sam Wanyanga
Siaya, October 2017

INTRODUCTION

In my memoir *From My Heart* I highlighted Pastor Silfano Ayayo Mijema's life history. I mentioned briefly his attributes, mainly his courage and the struggle he waged for our people. I indicated that what I had written about him was not his full life history and that one day his memoir would be compiled for future generations to read. That day has come. In consultation with his surviving family, and as a result of my research and the fruitful interviews and conversations I had with him before he passed away, I'm weaving his life history. Readers will now have an insight into the inspiring life of one considered by his people to be a true hero.

Pastor Silfano Ayayo Mijema led an exceptional life. He was ordained a pastor of the Seventh-day Adventist Church at a tumultuous time in the history of Central Kavirondo. He distinguished himself as talented leader. He was an astonishing pastor. He was thirty-seven years old at ordination, just out of the Anglican Church (Church Missionary Society), where he was neither allowed to preach nor teach though he was trained in both. In spite of his troubles with the Anglican Church's leadership, he opted to continue to serve the Lord and to help his people. Nothing was going to stop him. As long as the Lord wanted him to serve Him, as long as his people wanted him to lead despite the financial constraints and turbulent times, he was willing and ready to do what the Lord gave him the wisdom and strength to do.

As a Christian, he was persistent, determined and committed. To some he was tough, stubborn and even exacting, but he needed these attributes because he required the same degree of excellence from himself as he expected from others.

He was one of the most sympathetic Christian leaders of his time, but lack of preserved accounts of the achievements of the leaders of his era, caused by illiteracy and language barrier, made people hear little or nothing at all about him. In this book, his life and leadership style is told. His story contains refreshing inspiration, struggle and eventual success.

Pastor Silfano Ayayo Mijema earned the respect of not only the flock he ministered to but also of his fellow pastors and evangelists as well. When the story of how the Seventh-day Adventist Church came and spread in Kenya is written, even the General Conference of the Seventh-day Adventist Church will acknowledge Pastor Silfano Ayayo Mijema's contribution and leadership. He continually sought greater knowledge from the Bible, which enabled him to scale greater heights of attainment. Since the good news of the coming Saviour had not penetrated many parts of the world, Africa in particular, the success story of Pastor Silfano Ayayo Mijema in bringing the Seventh-day Adventist Church in Central Kavirondo, against great odds, should be looked at keenly by missionaries and evangelists aspiring to embark on global evangelization. His story and the success stories of others like him need to be told and retold in Kenya and wherever people need the inspirational example of outstanding leadership. Perhaps this style of leadership will one day be infectious and spread widely.

I hope that by reading this book, Pastor Silfano Ayayo Mijema's story of courage, inspiration and success will fire you up to be the very best Christian or responsible citizen. His captivating struggle to find a spiritual home for his people was timely. The earthly trials and troubles he underwent and surmounted were overwhelming. His decision to leave his peers, lifelong friends and his homestead, which he left to missionaries, was not only courageous but also audacious. His leadership style of *comply ask questions later* earned him admirers among his peers and the persons he worked with. His unique abilities and accomplishments can be attributed to his personal determination and drive. His humility and morality can be attributed to his relationship with and love for his God. He was a man who lived a life dedicated to service. That is the rich legacy of faith he left behind.

1

BIRTH

> *"For I know the plans I have for you," declares the LORD, "plans to prosper you and not harm you, plans to give you hope and a future..." Jer. 29:11 (NIV)*

It was a morning like any other in the African countryside. There was an overcast cloud, but this was not because it was about to rain; it was because there had been showers the night before and there were drizzles still.

My father, Nickolao Wanyanga, who had been born much earlier, remembered this day vividly, because on this day there was going to be merriment and dining—just short of feasting—in the village and teens like them were looking forward to sharing in the joys. People were still steeped deep in tradition. If it were not for the famine called *Choka*, which was ravaging the country at the time, there would have been local beer brewed by expert women of the village for the elderly men to drink, to honor the occasion. And during those days beer was consumed by elderly persons—and to some extent women, but only under special conditions.

While men drank sitting on their traditional stools, women would only drink sitting on the floor, at the feet of their brothers'-in-law. Young men and young women were forbidden to drink. My father told me that the young people would, however, circumvent this rule by convincing their mothers to give them beer without the elders' knowledge. But not his mother, he said, she feared his father!

It was a day indeed. White men had just arrived in this part of Africa, my father recalled, and there were rumors of the sighting of these strange people in parts of the country. According to my father, opinion was divided between those who wanted to see them and those who didn't. Those who didn't feared that their presence in the country would bring bad omen and cited the famine devastating the land at the time as an example.

"We will fight them if they come," they said.

But the other group was of the view that these people, strangers as they were, and strange as they looked, would bring good tidings. They strongly believed that their arrival would stop the ravages of *Choka* so that the people could once again prosper. They would not allow their colleagues to hurt the white men if and when they came.

Our people had been settled in this part of the country for close to one hundred years. They did peasant farming. They reared cattle, goats and sheep and raised poultry and even quails. Maize had not been introduced in this part of the country. People cultivated millet, finger millet (sorghum), simsim, green peas, cassava, sweet potatoes and other African crops. From the cows' milk they extracted ghee, which they used for cooking. There were no other cooking oils.

They used milk mainly for drinking when taking cooked cassava, sweet potatoes and sometimes *Kuon* (*Ugali* – the African equivalent of bread). Milk could be drunk fresh or sour. Milk became sour when it was left to stay over a period of time. And

Birth

to prevent germs and maggots from infesting it, they poured just the right quantity of a bull's urine to preserve it. This worked effectively.

There were no ploughs, harrows or even *jembes* to aid them in farming. They used crude, but efficient African tools like traditional hoes, *ratong'* (slashers) and *le* (axes). These items were crude in their shape and design, but effective and efficient nonetheless. They served the purpose for which they were made. This was the time of survival of the fittest. There were constant clan wars, which decimated large populations of people. Each clan fought other clans, and among the same clan—or even the same village—there was peer wrestling, which was actually violent. There were molesters as well. These were people whose preoccupation was to make life difficult for the less fit. They could beat one up, harass one and literally confine one within the precincts of his father's homestead.

Then there was the sadist. This was a guy who could dig up an anthill to expose the ants and hold one naked on the ants to bite while enjoying and laughing himself silly. Talk about evil! And the night runner. This was a guy possessed by strange devils, which only came alive in him at night. The devils would force him to strip naked and run around at night, kicking people's doors and harassing those walking at night. Other than wild animals, this was the next most feared 'species'.

Salt, as we know it today, had not been introduced. In the place of salt they used the ashes of burnt bean husks or burnt papyrus grass. There was no refined sugar in their diet. They chewed sugarcane, ate pawpaw, mangoes, oranges and other sweet fruits, which were abundant in the country at the time, as substitute for sugar. Their diet comprised mainly vegetables.

Cabbage and spinach had not been introduced in the area, but other African vegetables like leafy kales (*bad maro*), cowpeas (*boo*) korchoris (*mto*), black nightshade (*osuga*), Wondering Jew (*odielo*), amaranthus (*omboga*), devil's witchweed (*akeyo*) and many other varieties of African vegetables, some of which were actually medicinal, were widely used and relished. They did not have dishes, plates and the chinaware we boast of today. In the place of a plate they had a small basket (*ogudu*), and for a dish or bowl they had a feature made from clay called *tawo*. Their cooking pans were pots and they used firewood on hearths to cook.

Matches were unheard of. Fire was lit the traditional way—by rubbing two planks of special wood against each other until fire was produced. Once fire was started, putting a heap of dry cow dung on the glowing, burned firewood preserved it. This way, fire was preserved forever if it could be prevented from being rained on and dry cow dung added whenever it was about to burn out.

***

The birth of Ayayo Mijema in 1906 was indeed a day to remember. Even the heavenly hosts must have been happy. His father Mijema and mother Akumu must have been very happy. His elder brother Dulo must have been happy too.

This was an era when there were no trained doctors, nurses or even midwives, as we know them today. But the African women of that time had among them women knowledgeable in helping expectant mothers to deliver. Their tools of trade were water and a blade made from maize or millet stalk. They used the blade in cutting the umbilical cord and water to test if the baby was alive or dead. They poured cold water on the baby and if it didn't cry they knew it was dead.

Ayayo, born at that time, must have undergone a similar experience. A blade from maize or millet stalk must have cut

Birth

his umbilical cord. Although everybody was happy, little Ayayo did not know that he would live a hellish and turbulent life, sprinkled with sparse comfort here and there. Yet upon his birth came into this world a baby who was destined to grow to be a great man, a hero and the deliverer of a whole tribe (clan).

Pastor Silfano Ayayo Mijema's family tree

This is Pastor Silfano Ayayo Mijema's family tree as per available history.

MANI
↓
NDEREMA
↓
WASONGA
↓
WAMBOGA
↓
WAGA
↓
SINANI
↓
WASIANDIRA
↓
MAHUDHI
↓
LUGULU
↓
MIJEMA
↓
MIJEMA

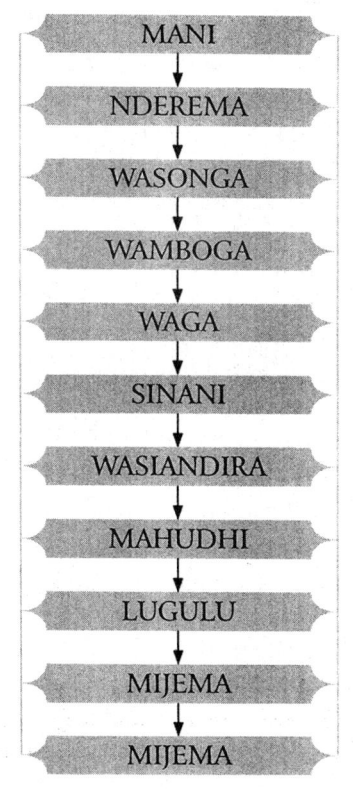

At the time Ayayo was born, naming of babies was strictly the preserve of the father, with the mother playing a supplementary role. So when the baby was born to Mijema and Akumu, Mijema named him Ayayo, in honor and remembrance of his deceased first wife, Ayayo. Mijema and Ayayo had three sons, Ogola, Wandago and Obingo, and one daughter, Owala. Ogola would later marry Auma and the couple would have four sons—Thuthu, Mayienga, Mijema and Ohon—and one daughter, Ogero.

Mijema's marriage to Akumu was his second, after he lost his first wife, Ayayo, through the cruel hand of death. Akumu, who was the daughter of Oyugi, of Uyoma Kokwiri, in Siaya County, was first married to Opapa Dulo, of Asembo Kabondo. She had three children with Opapa: Nyangolo the eldest, Naaman Dulo and a daughter, Yamo. Opapa had an elder brother named Owuor, who was jealous and never liked him. Owuor's jealousy manifested when Kokwiri people came to Asembo to perform a traditional ceremony, referred to in the local language as *lupo*. During this ceremony, food, livestock, cereals and other presents were brought from the wife's maiden home to her marital home to be consumed by people in her marital home. Kokwiri people came with a lot of food, including four head of cattle. This triggered the envy of Owuor. At that time Owuor lived with Opapa in one home, which belonged to Owuor.

As the Kokwiri people approached the home ululating, singing and dancing to fulfil the said ceremony, Owuor, raging with envy, blocked and locked the gate to prevent the ingress of the guests. This enraged the host, Opapa, who, in a stupor, wrestled and knocked Owuor down, broke the gate and let in his guests. In that moment, seeds of enmity between the two brothers were planted and would endure. As a result of the incident, Owuor started devising ways of finishing Opapa, including witchcraft.

Birth

When Opapa was later pricked and injured by a sharp object on the knee, it was claimed it was as a result of a spell of witchcraft placed on Opapa by Owuor. Opapa eventually died as a result of that very injury he had sustained and was buried in Kabondo, in Asembo.

Nyangolo, Dulo and Yamo survived him. Before Opapa died, he had advised his wife, Akumu, to leave Asembo as soon as possible after his death lest their children be bewitched. He advised her to go to her maternal uncle's home in Magombe, in Yimbo. These were the days when the wars between Uyoma people and the colonizing white men were raging. Meanwhile, Mijema who had also lost his wife and was a widower became a shrewd businessman. He sent traditional *jembes* (hoes) to Uyoma from Gem. In one of Mijema's trade missions to Uyoma, he visited Alomba and Odede, who were Akumu's relatives and were great friends with Mijema. In their conversation, Akumu's name featured. Mijema was told that Akumu was a very good singer, but was a widow. So Mijema requested them to talk to Akumu to find out if she could become his wife—since both of them had lost their spouses. A betrothal meeting was arranged, where the agreement was sealed and a date agreed on when Akumu would go to Gem.

Later, after receiving directions to Mijema's home in Gem, Akumu left for Gem with her daughter, Yamo. On her way there, she got lost and ended up in Regea, in Gem. Her baby fell sick on the way, overcame by heat and thirst and passed on. A Good Samaritan offered her a burial site, where she buried her child. It was a bitter blow to her. She did not only lose her daughter, but also that rendezvous with her fiancé. The Good Samaritan in her home gave her temporary shelter, after she had narrated to them her predicament. She did not, however, disclose to them the purpose of her journey. As she continued to stay in the homestead pondering what to do to meet her fiancé, she eventually told them she was on a mission to see Mijema.

Meanwhile word had reached Uyoma that Akumu had lost her way and that her child had died. Instead of directing her to Mijema's home, they conspired to dispatch her further into Kisa land, where they planned for her to be married to a widower, who was related to one of the women in the homestead.

The following day, very early in the morning, she was asked to accompany six women to Kisa to buy sorghum. She obliged and the group set off for Kisa. On arrival, their hosts received them warmly. Later that night she was separated from the women she had accompanied and was led to another house, where she spent the night with another woman. In the morning she did not see the women and never saw them again. On inquiring, she was told that the women had accomplished their mission and had headed back to Gem. That she was there to be remarried! Realizing that her protests would be futile, she decided to beat them at their own game. After all, the best way to extinguish a fire is to light another fire in the opposite direction and the two fires burn themselves out. So she cooperated with them in everything except the consummation of the marriage. She did the cooking, the dishes, collection of firewood and fetching of water, all the while plotting her escape.

So one day, on one of her missions to collect water, she decided to make good her plot to escape. She slipped into the bush and made her way as fast as she could to a river separating Kisa and Gem and crossed it by canoe after paying the coxswain a necklace. She made her way to Regea, to the home where she was offered temporary board. The woman who had arranged to have her married in Kisa was surprised to see her back. Then the Uyoma people, who had heard of Akumu's tribulations, made

Birth

their way to Regea to mourn Yamo and bring Akumu home. Although they did not find Akumu, they were warmly received and were told that Akumu had found a new husband in Kisa. The following day they were surprised when Akumu arrived at the home and a few minutes later Mijema arrived, fuming and spoiling for a fight. The presence of Uyoma people calmed him down, after which a meeting of elders was convened to discuss the matter of Akumu's alleged marriage to the Kisa man.

After ascertaining that Akumu's alleged marriage was never consummated, they decided to give Mijema his fiancée. Everybody was overwhelmed with joy: the home people, because they avoided a fight at their home and a possible lawsuit; Mijema, because he had finally found his fiancée; the Uyoma people, because their daughter had maintained the discipline they taught her and never compromised her trust and faithfulness to her fiancé; and Akumu, because she had at last found the man she had journeyed through the hostile wilderness, even losing her beloved daughter in the process, to meet. That was how Akumu married Mijema!

***

Of the three Opapa children, only Dulo survived. Nyangolo died under mysterious circumstances when he returned from the Army, where he had been drafted in the year 1914. He had come back to mourn the death of one of his nephews. Yamo, of course, died young in the arms of Akumu as she went to Gem to look for Mijema.

The sages say, "Once bitten twice shy!" Mijema, having lost Ayayo early in the marriage, was not going to wait for fate to land him in another quagmire of having to stay without a wife in case the fate Ayayo met befell Akumu. So he took another

Triumph Through Faith

wife, Agola, the daughter of Oyugi. She was Akumu's sister. This marriage did not work and they soon separated.

As noted earlier, Akumu had two sons and one daughter, namely Nyangolo, Naaman Dulo and Yamo, by a previous marriage. This second marriage was blessed with one son, Silfano Ayayo, and two daughters, Nyangolo and Okuom. Dulo married Bethseba Akoth, the stepsister to Azenath Ngalo, and the couple was blessed with a son, Nahor Odhiambo, and a daughter, Zipora Akumu, who, in adulthood, married Derick Nyawara.

Nahor married Maritha Anyango and were blessed with five sons: Phinehas Otieno, Seth Dulo, Isaiah Odiwuor, Silfano Ayayo and Jason Ochieng. They also had six daughters: Dorca Atieno Ogidi, Queen Elizabeth Odira, Ruth Adhiambo Joseph, Grace Anyango Michura, Gladys Akony Obonyo, and Teresa Owuonda Odhiambo.

Upon Bethseba's death, Dulo married Dinah Omolo, with whom he got one daughter, Christine Adhiambo. Upon Dulo's death, Dinah was inherited by Mudhune, with whom she got three daughters: Esther Awino, Mary Akoth and Yuanita Adongo. After Mudhune's death, Dinah migrated to South Nyanza, where she married Magidha, with whom she got two sons: Caleb Otieno and Joshua Ouma.

Because of posterity worries, Mijema later married Ojwando, with whom he got one daughter, Gladys Odiaga, the mother of Edwin Ochieng' On'gowo, Malachi Omondo On'gowo, Felgona Anyango, Margaret Tabu and Seline Awino.

Ayayo's other stepbrother, Wandago, married Ludia Nyawire, and were blessed with two sons, Odongo and Owino. Ludia was a sister to Anna Manyuru, who was married to Robert Ogola, with whom she had one son, Anania Ataro, and a daughter, Ogero. Anania married Clarise Sirega and begot one son,

Birth

Professor Edwin Omondi Ataro. Wandago married a second and a third wife, namely Apondi and Ojiwa, with whom he had daughters who died young.

While still young, his father joined a group of people who, as a result of ethnic persecution, moved to Kakamega, where they stayed for some time then returned to their original area when a semblance of peace was restored. Later, his father moved to Nyahera for the same reason and again returned for the same reason. At about this time, they had, as neighbours, the Kagola, who were welcomed and stayed with Waudi of Umswa clan and later stayed in the homes of Wasumwa and Lihunga, both Umanians. They lived with the Walgano, who were their cousins, Usuha, their distant cousins, and the Ndagaria people, who were found on this land. Ndagaria people's ancestor, Andali, stayed so peacefully with neighbours that Gem was known as Gem Andare—Andare being an adulterated form of Andali.

The other families that moved out of Masawa (Gem) to Kakamega with Mijema, to escape persecution and the oppression directed at them by the chief of the time and his ruling clan, were: Jason Mrego–Umani, Ofinyo Wamwai–Usuha, Muhwana–Umani, Lala–Umani, Ayugi Ochieng'–Umani, Obiero Wanderma–Umani, Jaramba Aremo–Umani, Jatan'g Wayara–Ndagaria, Olek Abondo–Usula, Oyamo Udhandha–Umoya, Wandiga Abala Aduda–Usuha, Ndong'a Mulure–Umgore, Sawanda Walgwe–Umgore, Ugali–Ulugano, Unyonje Lihanda–Ulugano and many more whose names cannot be remembered. Quite a good number of these families returned when the government clamped down on the persecutions and oppressions. A good number, however, remained in Shweywe, in Kakamega, where they continued to live peacefully with the brothers they found there. They still reside there today.

Triumph Through Faith

Mijema, the father of Ayayo, was among those who came back from Shweywe.

Mijema was indeed a no nonsense man. He was harsh, bold and confrontational. He never shied away from a fight and never let go once a fight was started until he defeated the foe or the foe defeated him. If someone offended him he would shout and curse till evening. He would stop only when he went to bed. He was feared and nobody wanted to pick a quarrel or a fight with him. He was a good fighter too, my father could recall. It was not surprising that he was known by the pseudonym *Tel Tel*—an African bird that makes noise most of the time; the woodpecker, in English. He was, however, disciplined, industrious, contented and committed to whatever he set out to do. Some of these attributes would help shape the life of his son, Ayayo, whom he passed them on to.

2

GROWING UP

For this very reason, make every effort to add to your faith goodness; and to goodness, knowledge; and to knowledge, self-control; and to self-control, perseverance; and to perseverance, godliness; and to godliness, brotherly kindness; and to brotherly kindness, love. For if you possess these qualities in increasing measure, they will keep you from being ineffective and unproductive in your knowledge of our Lord Jesus Christ. 2 Peter 1:5-8 (NIV)

History teaches us that many of the world's greatest people had very humble beginnings. They were ordinary people with an extraordinary amount of determination. They grew among their peers with the least suspicion or expectation that one day they would be great. Later in life, they surprised friend and foe by the sheer depth of their talent and achievement.

Ayayo grew up a healthy and robust child despite the fact that there were no prenatal and post-natal services. Children of that era were not vaccinated against any disease, my father recalled. But they survived nonetheless, courtesy of the diet and people who were knowledgeable in traditional medicine.

He played, like any other kid, with other children, including my father. They played hide and seek, made artefacts from mud, played soccer and wrestled. They also made toys they called fliers by boring a hole on a piece of blade of maize stalk about six inches in length and placing a piece of paper two inches in size at the ends of the blade opposite each other. The blade was then fixed loosely on the tip of maize or millet stalk and prevented from flying off by sticking mud on the tip of a small stick which the blade rotated on. They then ran with it against the wind, making the blade rotate. The faster one ran, the faster the blade rotated. It was fun. For soccer, they used *otange*, fruit of an African plant, which they kicked around. Indians brought tennis balls, which replaced *otange*, much later. From *otange* they made toy lorries and trailers long before lorries pulling trailers appeared on the roads. My dad recalled that Ayayo made the first toy trailer of this kind.

Ayayo grew up among children who walked naked since there were no clothes then. The youngest among them, ages two to ten, stayed stark naked. From eleven years upward, kids wore *ang'wola*—a piece of cloth fastened to a strap tied around the waist and placed between the rumps to cover the vital parts in front. The adult had a piece of hide fastened to a strap on the waist to cover the front part. This was what they had to cover their nakedness. As they walked along, the hide was either in front or behind, depending on circumstances. If someone were approaching from the front along the way, one would pull the hide in front to cover his vital parts. As he walked past, he pulled it to his back to cover the rump. Through the courtesy of the elders, it is known that even when a man went to visit his father-in-law's homestead, this was the attire he put on. It was only with the coming of white men and Indians that clothes, as known today, appeared on the scene and people started using them. There were no shoes or blankets. For blankets they used cattle hides to lie on and cover themselves as well. Bathing was discretionary, but some parents insisted that their kids bathe.

Growing up

And since there was no soap, bathing comprised mainly of dipping in water, rubbing one's body with a rod—and a split *otange* acting as soap—or a rough small stone, until one felt clean.

As a teenager, Ayayo was involved in activities that were engaged in by his age mates. Herding of cattle was a must, whether one's parents had cattle or not. If one's parents didn't have cattle, he helped look after an uncle's. Herding was fun and young people liked it. It gave them an opportunity to watch bulls fight, rams smash into each other's head, and goats, particularly he-goats, test their horns on each other. They also had the opportunity to socialize and make friends. Since they shepherded, they had time for playing soccer and practicing wrestling, which was vital for their defense. Wrestling techniques were not only for defense, wrestling itself was the sport of the day.

Being that *Jo-Umani's* source of livelihood was and still is farming, Ayayo, like his peers, engaged in farming activities. He ploughed with oxen, tilled, planted, weeded and harvested crops. He also helped with threshing and winnowing. Crops, once threshed and winnowed, were stored in a granary. A granary was made entirely from local materials. Not a single nail was used. It was all twines, small rod-like trees or reeds and ropes, made from sisal or the bark of certain local trees. The roof was made of reeds woven together using ropes and thatched with *osinde*—an African grass. The store was a cylindrical structure three feet wide and six feet high. It was suspended from the ground about one foot, resting on four stones placed at the four corners. The roof, once thatched, had to be lifted by a group of four strong men and placed on top of the structure. That structure was well ventilated to allow air in and out. It was also used as an ingress and egress by whoever wanted to retrieve something from the granary. Houses were built using similar technology except that the roof was woven on top of the structure and then thatched with grass. The door of the house was either a mat or a cylindrical structure, which was not strong enough to prevent anybody from getting into the house, except perhaps the dogs, skunks and jackals.

At the age of fourteen Ayayo was ready to be initiated into adulthood? properly. He was ready for his six lower teeth—two canines and four incisors—to be removed. The procedure was simple once one made up his mind to go through with it. Usually, in any area, there were just one or two people who had the technical knowledge of removing teeth. One had to arrive at the home of the expert before sunrise for the procedure to be completed before 9:00 a.m. The procedure had to be undertaken in the morning for health reasons. One, this guy was not a doctor and had no anesthesia to help his patient cope with the pain. Two, he had no knowledge of stopping loss of blood. He had to work in the morning when the temperatures were still low so that Mother Nature could help stop the inevitable bleeding. For medicine to stop bleeding, he chewed the leaves of some shrubs, squeezed water from them and smeared the resultant stuff on the wound where the teeth had just been removed. Remarkably, nobody bled to death as a result of the procedure.

After the procedure, one went straight to the home of birth of his mother, where the brothers of the mother (uncles) gave him gifts, chief among which was a hen. That was the uncles' way of giving wealth to their nephews. The nephew was expected to take good care of the hen. From the hen the nephew was expected to raise chicks and therefore more hens, which he was expected to sell and buy a goat. Later he would sell the goat's offspring and acquire a heifer, which would also produce offspring, which he would use to pay dowry. This was one of the motivations

Growing up

that pushed young people to remove their lower teeth as they viewed it as a path to acquisition of wealth. Even though both genders had their teeth removed the brothers would pay dowry with whatever wealth a daughter's hen generated. The daughter though would also use the wealth to take care of her needs.

In their wisdom, our forefathers came up with this idea to help tetanus (lockjaw) victims get food down their gullets while undergoing treatment. It later stuck and became a symbol of maturity and a gateway to adulthood. Historians know that there was an era when a decent girl or boy could not court a girl or a boy who had not removed her or his lower teeth. It even became a mark by which the Luos were identified.

The practice, however, was not restricted to Luos. This mutilation of body parts was rampant among virtually all the tribes of Kenya. Some tribes removed two lower incisors, others one. The Luhyas, like the Luos, removed six teeth. Others mutilated their ears, genitals, and other parts of the body. In the 1950s, however, young people started shunning the practice of teeth removal as a result of which you can today hardly find a Luo or a Luhya with teeth removed. Many tribes are moving away from female genital mutilation too. Like the young men of his teenage days, Ayayo got his teeth removed and lived without them for the rest of his life. He had to bow to culture.

Ayayo lived his teenage years when entertainment was restricted to *bodi* (a set of African musical instruments comprising a wooden box and a round metal six inches in diameter; *nyatiti* (an African musical instrument with eight strings stretched horizontally in an open frame and played by pulling the strings); *ohangla* (a set of African musical instruments comprising a number of drums varying in sizes placed vertically and played by beating upon them with batons); and *orutu* (an African one-stringed musical instrument played by rubbing against it with another string tied to a bow like structure). These were the types of musical gadgets that entertained Ayayo and his peers when he was growing up. More often than not, they were played at funerals and post-funeral ceremonies. Guitars, accordions and gramophones were additions to the African music that came later, with the piano being one of the very last entrants into the African music world.

Ayayo was lucky he was not a twin. In his days twins were considered a bad omen. Woe unto them if they were the first-born. If one had the 'misfortune' of having twins before any other child, family members and villagers insisted that the twins be killed. Most twins met their fate this way and within a few hours of birth. Christianity and modernity, however, have since wiped out this archaic practice. For other twin births, there was a lot to be done or not done. Ceremonies abounded. There was nothing that could be done to or for one twin and not the other. If it was fetching water or firewood, they went together. If it was going out to pluck vegetables, they went together. Cooking, bathing, sleeping, they were together. The twin that was born first was named Opiyo, if it was a son or Apiyo, if a daughter. The one that followed was named Odongo or Adongo depending on the gender. Luos generally give their children a name with a first-letter "O" for males and an "A" for females. There are, however, a few exceptions to this rule. But the naming of children using Luo names was and still is so contagious that *Jo-Umani* adopted it wholesale. They name their children the way Luos do to date.

If one of the twins died, the surviving twin was not supposed to know. Parents and elders tried their best to conceal the death. If for some reason circumstances were such that they would not, they ensured the surviving twin never saw the dead twin or his tomb.

Growing up

If a parent of twins died, the twins were taken away from the homestead because they were not supposed to see the corpse and the tomb. Once the burial ceremony was finalized, the tomb was covered completely before the twins would be allowed back home. The tomb would remain covered until grass grew and covered it.

This was Ayayo's world!

***

The First World War broke out in 1914, when Ayayo was only eight years old. He could not be conscripted into the army. He had, however, stared danger in the face when he lived through the great famines. These famines had names given by the locals. The first to ravage the country was called *choka*, also known as *odila*. This struck in 1906, when Ayayo was a baby. At the end of the war the country experienced another major famine, *keya*, in 1918-1919, named after the soldiers in the First World War—KAR (Kings African Rifles). In 1921 the country went through another famine—*chwe kode* (continue with it). It was named so because it was as if it was a prolonged version of *keya*. In 1927 yet another famine ravaged the country—*kee dede* (famine of locusts). The ravaging effects of locusts that struck during that year caused this famine. Locusts struck again in 1930, causing a famine called *Osodo*. In 1932 there was a famine, *nyangweso*, which also ravaged the country. In 1943 there was yet another famine, *ladhri*, probable cause being the Second World War. The peak of the war was in 1943, when the United States of America had just been forced into the war by Japan. There were other famines like *ondonga*, *otuoma*, *abwao* and *ong'iyo*. There was also another big famine named *nduswe*, which was caused by drought. It caused mass livestock deaths.

Triumph Through Faith

Apart from famines, Ayayo survived inter-clan wars, diseases and plagues. He survived these tribulations because he had God as his protector. God had a critical mission He was preparing Ayayo for. He escaped polio, tetanus, cholera, typhoid, bubonic plague and leprosy. The latter was highly contagious. Anybody infected could not mingle with other people. The infected person was removed from the home, tied with a long rope, then taken to a bushy area or near a river or stream, tied to a tree and left there to die. Another rope would be tied on the tree and pulled away from him as far as it could stretch. This would be the person's feeding line. Food would be taken to him by tying it on the rope and alerting him to pull. The utensils used were never retrieved. This would be the routine until he died. Death could come quickly or slowly. It could come quickly if wild animals devoured him or slowly if he lived his remaining life. After death, his body was left out there for wild animals to feast on.

Rats transmitted bubonic plague. It was fatal. It killed so many people that the colonial government got worried and devised a method of eradicating the rats. The government instructed the people to kill rats and bring their tails to the offices. If one brought twenty tails, for example, government officials knew twenty rats were dead and they would give credit of up to 20% on tax liability. People fell for it and in no time rats died in hundreds of thousands and the plague dissipated. It never recurred. These calamities—famines, diseases, plagues and wars— decimated large populations of people and even caused migrations of villagers and communities. But through it all, God was with Ayayo. Like the Israelites of old, he was kept under God's wings.

As a teenager, he was a good soccer player. Soccer balls had been brought by Indian traders and teenagers and adults learnt

Growing up

how to play. Ayayo was not left behind. He learned quickly and later became an expert. He was also an athlete who excelled in the sprints. He would not, however, get anywhere with these activities because there were no organized leagues nor competitions where he could prove his prowess.

His other talents would later show elsewhere.

He and his peers had to contend with the many mad men and mad women who wreaked havoc in the villages. These people were feared and nobody dared confront them. They were never known to kill, but they beat people up. At the time Ayayo grew up, they could block the main road leading to Yala and nobody would do anything about it. On market days they could move into the market and people ran helter-skelter, leaving their merchandise scattered all over the place. People returned only after they had left. These insane people feared one another; one would not come where the other was. It was as if they respected each other's territory. Male ones harassed their female counterparts by chasing them away. The female ones easily obliged to avoid confrontation. It worked like a rule.

Teenagers of Ayayo's time never dated. The elders strictly prohibited dating. The girls deeply respected their parents and would not play along. Christianity had not taken root in earnest, but this was an area where African cultural traditions were in consonance with Christian teachings. Teens would, however, interact freely since this was one of the ways they identified possible brides. The other way was through intermediaries. A relative of the groom, who would later become the intermediary, identified a bride. After identification, the matter was reported to the groom and bride's parents. The two parties would then arrange a betrothal meeting (meeting of the parents of the bride and the groom), where bride price was discussed and agreed upon. Once an agreement was struck, the groom's father released the bride price, which consisted of several head of cattle and in some places a goat or two. Meanwhile, the intermediary would arrange for the bride-to-be to meet and see her man, possibly at the intermediary's home or house. And even before the formalities of paying dowry were completed, the groom-to-be would arrange with strong boys of the village to pull the bride-to-be from her home, mostly under the cover of darkness. What happened after cannot be covered here as it may form a book on its own. The modern come-we-stay is a close relative of this pull-we-stay arrangement. Crude, it seems now, but a lot of fun it was then!

3

PASTOR SILFANO'S FAMILY

He who finds a wife finds a good thing, And obtains favor from the LORD. Prov. 18:22 (NKJV)

In 1925, Silfano met and fell in love with Asenath Ngalo. Asenath was the daughter of Owiti wuod Oburu also known as Owiti Ong'wana, one of the elders of Kagola clan, in Gem. She was the first child of Mr Owiti through his younger wife Merab Aduol. Owiti was already married to Merab's elder sister, Orem nyar Oganda from Boro. It was not unusual that sisters would marry the same man in those days. Merab's brothers were Jason Wahore and Joseph Otieno. She also had one sister, Sibia Rogo. Her older stepbrothers were Padre Reuben Omulo and James Aweyo. Stepsisters older than her were Pricilla Odera, and twins Doris Nyando and Bathsheba Akoth Adongo.

It is believed that Bethseba's marriage to Naaman Dulo, the stepbrother of Silfano Ayayo, made Asenath's marriage to Silfano possible. Asenath and Silfano had a wedding in 1925 at the Ulumbi Anglican Church, which was presided over by Padre Reuben Omulo.

Triumph Through Faith

Asenath's parents were a lovely and lively family as they were good Christians. Her family embraced Anglicanism at its inception in the region. They never got involved in the ethnic intrigues of their kinsmen, who were out to annihilate Ojwando people. If you are patient and read through this story of the life of Silfano, you will learn that one of the uses of history should be to discipline our emotions and actions—both covert and overt—with knowledge; and to teach us to conduct and solve our controversies and differences in a civilized and dignified manner. This should not be missed.

Asenath was a woman of rare qualities indeed. She was a loving, tender and hardworking woman. She was polite and generous. She was a fitting and worthy partner and aide to Silfano. Behind every successful man there is a *real* woman. Asenath would stand by Silfano's side as a shield and defender for the rest of her life. Perhaps without her Silfano would not have become such a great man, revered by many. She was the rock upon which his greatness was anchored.

The one thing that stood her out as a dignified wife was her humility and love for her children. This will be manifested as Silfano's story unfolds. Suffice it to say for now that she was hardworking and ensured food was on the table for the family and the many guests, workers and relatives Silfano had to take care of. Above all, she was a faithful Christian. Her most valuable lessons were not in what she said, but in what she did and how she did it.

We are reminded in 1 Peter 4:16 thus: *However, if you suffer as a Christian, do not be ashamed, but praise God that you bear that name. (NIV)* All the sufferings and tribulations the Ayayos encountered and surmounted were because they were exemplary Christians. The Lord says this in Hebrews 13:5: *Never will I leave you, never will I forsake you.* The Lord kept His word. He never

Pastor Silfano's family

forsook the Ayayos. He never abandoned the Ojwandos. He never ignored their pleas for protection. Like the bright star in the wilderness during Israelites' exodus, he led the way. And like the bright star to the shepherds during Jesus' birth, He led the way and protected Silfano, his family, the Jo-Umani and all the Ojwando people. Like He did to Ishmael, He never abandoned the Ojuodhi people.

Silfano and Asenath were blessed with eight children, five boys and three girls. Let me mention them. Tobias Otieno, Mahalon Seme, Duncan Lich, ABC Ochola, Beldina Akeyo, Amos Ochieng, Joyce Akumu and Loice Anyango. Mahalon Seme and Duncan Lich died young and on the same day. The rest lived to adulthood.

His first son, **Tobias Otieno**, married Rosebella Njoga, the daughter of Mr William Ayodo and Mama Dursila Sawala. Rosebella's brothers and sisters were: Samuel Onyango Ayodo, Jonathan Onunga, Ezra Otieno, Mordicae Osano, Ludia Ojwan'g Okech, Mical Ndong'a Omom, Hulda Abong'o Oyugi, Judith Auma Okoyo, Damaris Osuri Ochola and Caren Atieno Adhanja. Her stepbrothers and stepsisters, through her stepmother, Mama Caren Ayodo, were: Hesbon Okoth, Eunice Atudo, Seth Otieno, Mary Achieng', Lilly Akinyi, Elisaphan Opiyo, Simon Ochieng and Musa Akuno.

God blessed Tobias and Rosebella with 9 children—6 boys and 3 girls. They were: Edwina Atieno, Martin Omondi, Stephen Ochieng, Dr Zachariah Ngalo Otieno-Ayayo, Paul Oluoch, Cleveland Okoth Ayayo, Christine Adhiambo, Rena Alberta and James Ayodo, all of whom are married and have children.

Edwina got married to James Ombado and their children are: June Akinyi Kimani, Jason Ombado, Daisy Ombado and Tobias Ombado.

June got married to Dr Martin Kimani. Martin got married to Viridiana and their children are: Rosebella Adhiambo Omondi and Tobias Mawasang'a Omondi. Martin had a son by a previous union. His name is Dennis Omondi. He is also married.

Stephen got married to Roselyne Atieno and their children are: Stephanie Singobellah, Flozil Noelle and Belorah Hazel. Dr Zachariah Ngalo got married to Susan Mellanie and their children are: Jordan Opondo, Sifa Njoga and Sraela Chiya.

Paul got married to Maria Orinda and their child is **Martha (Samara) Oluoch**.

Cleveland got married to Eresi Adhiambo and their children are: Ida Rose and Samson Geda.

Christine got married to Martin Odhiambo and their children are: Petty Bella, Dephnie, Asenath, Clare and Tobias (Hope) Emanuel.

Rena was married to her estranged husband, George Auko, and had one child, Catherine Auko.

James got married to Dorcas Adhiambo and their child is Musa YoSalem Ler.

The second son was **Prof. ABC Ochola**, who was married to Berith, with whom he got one child, Jenny Asenath. He later married Christina, with whom he had two children—Magaretta Akinyi and Erick Ocholla.

The third son was **Amos Ochieng'**, who was married to Nereah Adero, with whom he got seven children—two sons and five daughters. They were: Asenath Ngalo, George Okech, Dorcas Awino, Alice Adikinyi, Millicent Akoth, Beril and Silfano Ayayo. Nereah Adero was the daughter of Felix Shadrack Aloo and Alice Adikinyi. She had one brother, Joel Omondi, and five sisters, namely: Dorcas Atieno, Prisca Agola, Julia Akoth, Kiloi

Pastor Silfano's family

Johera and Grace Anyango.

The first daughter was **Beldina Akeyo**, who had the following children: Kenneth Ochieng, Hastings Odhiambo, Pamela Ngalo, Mabel Awino, Duncan Odipo, Edwin Oluoch, Jackline Odhiambo, Erick Odhiambo and Asenath Achieng'.

The Second daughter was **Joyce Akumu**, who was married to Johnson Ndira, with whom she had eight children: two sons and six daughters. They were: Jane Awuor, David Otieno, Mary Akinyi, Alice Atieno, Asenath Ngalo, Linet Ndira, Joseph Onyango and Roselyne Awino.

The third daughter was **Loice Anyango**, who married Peter Nyangulu, with whom she had one child called Beatrice Atieno.

Silfano and Asenath had the following great grandchildren at the time of writing this book: Beldina, Henry, Maryanne, Daniel Otieno, Lameck, Elvira Okuom, Beth Lavuli, Andrew Waggoner, Nevins Byington, Mariam Makeba, Geofrey Ongoro, Edwin Ocholla, Amos Ayayo, Audrey Sharolla, Arphaxad Xavier, Melanio Meale Fiona Nelly, Marlene Rose, Annette Ayayo, Richard Leech, Lavenda Atieno, Lorent Adhiambo, Sally Achieng', Nova Akoth, Amos Ayayo, Silvia Awino, Marion Atieno, Helfas Ajwang' and others.

That's the Asenath family tree! Silfano and Asenath lived happily until death of Asenath in 1959 made them part.

Silfano's second family

A family is a place where principles are hammered and honed on the anvil of everyday living. (Charles Swindell)

In 1962 Pastor Silfano tied the knot with **Miss Esther Achieng Oyieke**, at Nyaduon'g Seventh-day Adventist Church. Esther was the daughter of Mr Samuel Oyieke and Mrs Julia Muga. The marriage was blessed with eight children, seven boys:

Samuel Oyieke, Jacob Okoth, Thadayo Mijema, Moses Oswago, Jeremiah Ochieng, Elija Opondo and Jonathan Ogweno; and one daughter, Asenath Ngalo.

Esther was a strong woman and, having come from an Adventist home, had no difficulty fitting into the lifestyle of the Ayayos. She played her role as a wife to a pastor very well, helping him whenever she could. She became a good mother to her kids, sometimes playing the double role of mother and father as need arose. Pastor Silfano later aged as the years rolled by and could no longer discipline his children as he used to. Esther stepped into the void and effectively played both her role and his. These children have also been blessed and have families and prosperous lives. God blessed them and continues to bless them.

Esther has taken good care of Pastor Silfano's home, where she has continued to reside after his death. One of her sons, like all Asenath's sons, has built his own homestead; the remaining will do so soon.

Esther's first son, **Samuel Oyieke**, was married to Mary Atieno Oyieke, with whom he had one son and four daughters: Elijah Malkom Onyango Oyieke, Agnes Witney Achieng Oyieke, Everline Patience Awuor Oyieke, Gloria Akinyi Oyieke and Anjela Ayayo Oyieke.

Her second son, **Jacob Okoth**, was married to Irene Auma Okoth, with whom he had two daughters: Polly Akinyi and Esther Anyango.

The third son, **Thadayo Mijema**, married Benta Achieng, with whom he had two sons: John Ochieng and Silfano Ayayo.

The fourth son, **Moses Oswago**, married Christine Nyabonke Oswago, with whom he had four children: Jesseh Onyango, Micael Adhiambo, Silfano Ayayo and Sarah Achieng.

Pastor Silfano's family

The fifth son, **Jeremiah Ochieng**, got married to Jocinta Anyango Ochieng, with whom he had three daughters and one son: Esther Night Ayayo, Annette Akoth, Bill C. Ochieng and June Akinyi.

The sixth son, **Elijah Opondo**, was not married at the time of writing this book.

Her seventh son, **Jonathan Ogweno**, was married to Queensly Adhiambo Ogweno and had two daughters and one son: Rebecca Achieng Ogweno, Eunice Awino Ogweno and Cohen Ochieng Ogweno.

The only daughter, **Asenath Awuor**, was married to Dan Amayo and had the following children: Calvin Ayayo, Nixon Semedi, Nickol Macklean and Milan Nicktone.

That's the Esther family tree!

They should maintain the unity of the family, which Pastor Silfano strove to create, which he nurtured and bequeathed to his offspring, for posterity.

So Abraham said to Lot, 'Let's not have any quarreling between you and me, or between your herdsmen and mine, for we are brothers...' Gen 13:8 (NIV)

Those words of Abraham to Lot should be the words that will guide Pastor Ayayo's people into eternity!

4

LIGHT IN CHRISTIANITY

I call heaven and earth as witnesses today against you, that I have set before you life and death, blessing and cursing; therefore choose life, that both you and your descendants may live. Deut 30:19 (NKJV)

The Kenya-Uganda railway did not reach Kisumu until 1901, when it opened up the country from Mombasa to Kisumu. Before construction of the railway, it was hardly possible to travel from the coast of Kenya into the hinterland. Along the way lived fierce tribes like the Maasai, who made access impossible. Since Mombasa was the gateway to trade in the region, opening this railway unleashed great opportunities for European and Indian merchants. Indians, having taken part in the construction of the railway, discovered the potential for trade and advancement, which this country had. The country, particularly the hinterland, was still virgin—with rich arable land and a cool tropical climate suitable for farming and rearing cattle. The Indians saw opportunity to trade with the local people. Wherever the Europeans went to open up more space, the Indians were in tow. To their credit, I must say, they helped

Light in Christianity

in the civilization of our people. They brought items like sugar, salt, soap, clothes, shoes and other necessities of life.

This was an opportune time for the British, who had been given our country when Europeans partitioned Africa, to organize a system of governance for the African nations. We owe it to the British that the system of government they set up, although not perfect, helped stop inter-clan and inter-tribe wars, which were rampant at the time. Had the British not come at that time I would not be sitting here writing this book, because Ayayo would not have done what he did, which enabled me to be educated and enlightened. The bottom line is, I would not have been what I am today and Ayayo would never have become what he became. In their own way, the British saved us!

The first thing to be appreciated, which the British bequeathed to us, was education. They went out of their way to teach our forefathers and fathers how to read and write. They knew we could not progress unless we became literate. From them we got modern education, a modern lifestyle, and a modern system of government. We now eat our food on plates and dishes and not the earthenware and baskets that we used to eat our food from. We are grateful we have clothes and sleep on beds, mattresses, and under blankets and bed sheets instead of hides and skins of animals. But the greatest thing they gave us remains Christianity. I believe, without this, the British, and indeed other Europeans, would not have succeeded in colonizing Africa. Guns alone would not have succeeded. With guns they would have wiped out whole populations, leaving nobody alive to colonize or Christianize. Of course they might have opted for this, but having wiped out populations elsewhere they decided to give Africa a different approach. They used more Bibles than guns and succeeded. That's why we marry off our daughters and sons through weddings. We have our own missionaries traversing the whole world and have our pastors and evangelists in the service of the Lord.

In Western Kenya, where Ayayo was born, people worshipped various gods before white men brought us Christianity. Some worshiped the sun. Every morning (sunrise) and every evening (sunset) they prayed and offered sacrifices to the sun by beseeching it to rise and set with good tidings for them and their families. They offered sacrifices to these gods by way of chickens and quails and believed the sun heard and granted their supplications. Others believed in the power of magic and sorcery. There was nothing in this world, they believed, that magic or sorcery could not accomplish. They adored and worshipped it. Folks who had these magical powers were feared and whatever they said had to be obeyed. Luo history is replete with people who had such powers—Gor Mahia, Obondo Mumbo, Ogola wuod Ayieke and others. Others worshipped Were Nyakalaga, who was the unseen being with immense powers. This was the closest our people got to worship the living God. During Ayayo's era, before the white men came, these practices were rampant, but Christianity changed so much around us that those who still practice witchcraft and worship the sun are rare indeed.

Christianity, as handed to us, was adulterated with Western cultures, some of which were in direct conflict with African cultures. That, however, did not discourage Africans from embracing it. The first missionaries to penetrate Western Kenya were the Anglicans, through the Church Missionary Society (CMS), closely followed by the Roman Catholics (RC), the Seventh Day Adventists (SDAs) and others. Bishop J. J. Willis established a CMS mission in Maseno in 1906. Pastor Carscallen started a Seventh-Day Adventist mission in Gendia, in Rachuonyo District, about the same year. The earliest RC mission was established at Ojola, in Kisumu County, and

Light in Christianity

later spread to Yala and Ran'gala in Siaya County. In Ogada in Kisumu, and Nyabondo in Nyakach, Rev. Herbart Woolsey Irniss started an African Inland Mission (AIM). The Friends had Rev. Charlton, who opened a Quaker Mission in Kaimosi. The Pentecostals had Rev. Rees, who started a mission station in Nyangore. These were the pioneer churches, which established missions in Western Kenya at that time.

Ayayo, along with a good number of his people, joined the Anglican Church. The Anglican and the Roman Catholic churches were the pioneer churches in the area. Ayayo's people preferred the Anglicans because, in addition to teaching the Bible, they taught people how to read and write. They wanted as many people as possible to be literate so that they could have a pool of local literate people to train to be catechists, teachers, lay readers or even padres. RC, on the other hand, was interested in teaching recitals of church doctrines. They embraced all and sundry, as they did not mind whether one was a drunkard or a polygamist—things the other churches frowned on.

On his baptismal day, Ayayo was christened Silfanus, or Silfano, as the local people pronounced it. Christian (Biblical) names were given a twist by local people. David is *Daudi*, Matthew is *Mathayo*, Luke is *Luka*, Mark is *Mariko,* etc. A few exceptions are Samuel, Daniel, Ruth, etc. With Silfano in the Anglican Church, his people joined that church in droves, until they comprised a total of five churches in Gem: Malanga, Maliera, Lundha, Muhaka and Luanda. Thus Silfano's people were spiritually cared for, at least for that time. Little did they know that being in the Anglican Church would be the biggest mistake of their lives. I'll explain later.

Once in church, they started learning how to read. This was to enable them to read the only book that was available—the

Triumph Through Faith

Bible. Luckily it had been translated into Luo by the early missionaries, who themselves were not Luos but had learnt Luo well enough to be able to supervise the translation. People quickly became literate and started learning arithmetic and English as well. Silfano was at the forefront of this endeavor, and being a gifted person, he quickly mastered reading, writing, arithmetic and some English. He was on his way up.

Once his people embraced Christianity they never looked back. A sizeable number of them joined the Roman Catholic Church, but their story is outside the scope of this book. After joining the Anglican Church, Silfano rallied his people to the church. He succeeded in this. Most of his people stopped smoking bhang (*Cannabis sativa*) and sniffing tobacco. They used special smoking pipes for tobacco and bhang. They also drank a traditionally brewed alcohol called *busaa* in the local dialect. They cut off all that and even witchcraft by not embracing witches and sorcerers anymore. They became devoted Christians.

5

THE STRUGGLE

We need to be at peace with our past, content with our present, and sure about our future, knowing they are all in God's hand. (Joyce Meyer)

The first group of Ojuodhi people to come to Western Kenya was Kagola. Their son, named Rading', came and was welcomed. He had many sons, chief among them were: Sande, Ohon, Omoro and Odera. During that time, Jo-Umani leader was Wasumwa. Wasumwa and Rading' became great friends. It was believed that Rading' was a prolific medicine man, particularly with charms for war. He was consulted whenever warriors were going out for war. This is what made Wasumwa interested in him, because at that time wars were widespread and Wasumwa wanted to win all of them. It was Wasumwa who was instrumental in settling Rading' in Gem.

Wasumwa was related to and was a friend of Mumia's, who was the undisputed leader of the whole of Kavirondo, as it was then known. Kavirondo later became Nyanza, and this comprised the whole of Western Kenya, from Migori to Mt Elgon.

Triumph Through Faith

Later, when the British organized the government, Gem was allowed to stand on its own as a Location and there was need to appoint a chief. Sande Rading' was appointed the new chief of Gem.

Apart from being friends with Jo-Umani, Sande married daughters of Jo-Umani. Three of his wives were from Umani. He married Adero daughter of Thuma, Onjalo daughter of Sijenyi, and Adikinyi daughter of Sijenyi. Sande ruled with fairness and respect. He was fair to Jo-Umani and respected them. Jo-Umani also loved him as a son-in-law and as a fair leader. They had no issues or complaints against him or against Ojuodhi people. But this would last only as long as he ruled. Upon leaving office he overlooked his sons and recommended Ogada Odera, the son of his brother Odera Rading', to take over from him. Ogada Odera had no home of his own. He lived with his family in what was perceived to be Sande's home. But Sande's gesture to his nephew, Ogada, did not sit well with his own sons, particularly the elder son, Opiche, who, in his anger and indignation, rallied his brothers with whom he proceeded to burn down Ogada's houses and chased him away. Thus the new chief found himself homeless and on the street, so to speak. Ombonya, son of Lihunga, Ja-Umani and a great friend of Ogada, talked to his father, Lihunga, to allow Ogada to stay in their home. Lihunga agreed and Ogada and his family were permitted to build their houses in Lihunga's home. He lived in this home until he died and was buried there.

Ogada Odera married Ong'iyo, daughter of Njoni, from Umani. Unlike Sande before him, he did not show brother-in-law respect to Jo-Umani. He was arrogant, sly and oppressive. He lorded it over Ojwando people, particularly his in-laws, Jo-Umani, who he strove to make slaves of the Ojuodhi people. He conscripted them into the army with reckless abandon.

The struggle

Whether it was building of roads, prevention of erosion, clearing of bushes, carrying heavy loads from place to place, or building new camps, Ojwando people were the ones to do them. They were forced to do all the hard work. Their Ojuodhi counterparts were exempted, courtesy of Chief Ogada Odera. Ojwando people, of course, did not take these affronts sitting down. No dignified people could. To put things into perspective, consider that these people could not be leaders either in the church or on the secular front. They were not allowed space anywhere and were restricted to their tiny homesteads only. If this wasn't a recipe for a revolution, what was?

But wait. How about in the political realm?

Here too they were not allowed to participate, not even at the local level. They were excluded in all local representative bodies. They could not be members of the Local Native Council (LNC) or even the Locational Council (LC). They could be seen but not heard. Their tongues were tied, their lips sealed and there was no forum where they could air their grievances. Do you get a sense of how desperate things were for them?

Then Silfano came along!

This driven, visionary leader became their voice and hope. He taught them that whatever their needs were, Jesus was not only able, but was willing to assist them. Christ was going to lead and guide and defend them in times of trouble. They knew the Son of God was a supporter, a companion and a friend when lonely and needy people needed a shoulder to lean on. Silfano told them that Jesus was a motivator to help them move ahead even in times of deep trouble. They were emboldened by the enriching words of King David in Psalms number 23. Listen to the words:

The Lord is my shepherd, I shall not be in want. He makes me lie down in green pastures, he leads me beside quiet waters, and he restores my soul. He guides me in paths of righteousness for his name's sake. Even though I walk through the valley of the shadow of death, I will fear no evil for you are with me; your rod and your staff, they comfort me. You prepare a table before me in the presence of my enemies. You anoint my head with oil; my cup overflows. Surely goodness and love will follow me all the days of my life, and I will dwell in the house of the LORD forever. (NIV)

The Lord could not tolerate the injustices visited on Ojwando people. He was going to help them find an escape route. He was going to use Silfano to help them break the chain of bondage forever.

***

Silfano had no formal education. During his teenage years, there were no formal schools until churches started appearing on the scene. When the Anglicans reached the area and established churches, they started teaching people to read and write. Silfano seized this opportunity and learned both. He picked up English and arithmetic as well. He had a burning desire to become a teacher and strove to excel in his studies so that he could get the opportunity to train as a teacher. By now ethnic animosity between Ojwando people and those who ruled them had reached alarming proportions. He saw how his people were oppressed and denied education and wanted to do something about it.

But school had to be first.

The Anglicans had started a sector school in Malanga. This school was supposed to cater for the learning needs of Anglicans in the area. Since Ojwando people were Anglicans, Malanga Sector School was their school. Indeed, Ojwando children went to Malanga Sector School in big numbers. At the school,

The struggle

pupils learned from STD 1 to STD 3, then sat for the highly competitive Common Entrance Examination. Those who passed went to Maseno School for STD 4 to STD 8, then on to Alliance School. From Alliance, successful students proceeded to Makerere University, in Uganda, for either a diploma or a degree.

Silfano completed Sector School and, when an opportunity arose for training teachers and lay readers at the Butere Normal School, he and his friend from Usuha, Andrea Ochola, seized the opportunity. The church sent them to Butere Normal School. When they reported in 1934 for the two-year course, Silfano's name was not in the list of new entrants. He could not understand why his name was on the list that left Malanga, but was missing on the list that arrived in Butere. The white man who was the principal of the school immediately suspected foul play and contacted Archdeacon Owen, who solved the stalemate. This is what happened: Silfano's name had been deleted from the list sent to Butere. Eventually he was admitted and both he and Andrea Ochola successfully completed their training in 1935. They became qualified teachers and lay readers. They could teach in a sector school or minister in a church. You can imagine how happy they were. They were the only trained people at the time. Even the teachers, who taught at Malanga and Luanda Sector schools, the two Anglican primary sector schools in the area, were not trained. Silfano and Andrea were thus a cut above them all. This was bound to raise eyebrows. And it did. But let us come to that later.

In the 1930s the Anglicans trained one Nyende Aruwa, in Limuru, to be a priest. He was later ordained a padre and made to be in charge of the Gem Anglican churches. Earlier, Ogada Odera had assumed the chieftainship of the northern part of Gem, as Mumia no longer administered it, from Mumias. And

Triumph Through Faith

his uncle, Sande, had relinquished chieftainship. Nyende and Ogada Odera hatched a plot to deny Ojwando children education. They feared that if Ojwando children got education they would compete with Ojuodhi children and deny them advancement opportunities. Nyende and Ogada thus put in place a simple plot, which would not only deny Ojwando children education but also drive their parents away from church. It was thus not surprising that the Anglican Church, through Padre Nyende, barred Silfano and Andrea from either teaching in Anglican schools or ministering in Anglican churches.

The die was cast.

The people immediately started agitating for complete separation from the Jo-Kagola in churches, schools and administration. If you think this agitation was misguided, consider the cynicism of the two leaders, Nyende and Ogada. Their plan was two-pronged. First, they planted rascals on the road leading to the school. Their brief was to beat Ojwando children thus stopping them from going to school. And this became a daily routine. Some of Ojwando's brightest children dropped out of school. Those whose parents organized escort completed school, but when they sat the exams and passed, their names were deleted from the list and names of Jo-Kagola children who did not pass well were inserted to replace them. It was cynical and disgusting.

But I don't think you get it yet. Let me bring it home!

Imagine your son has performed well in a national examination. You have received the results and have even received a letter inviting him to the next level. You report with your son to the institution and for the first time you discover that his name is not on the list of the students to be admitted. Imagine you are there with full fees and have all the requirements you were

The struggle

instructed to put together. Can you see it? Suddenly his name is missing?

What happened? You ask indignantly.

You come to discover someone in authority deleted your son's name and replaced it with his son's. And the sad part is that he is also there with his son checking in. His son was in the same school with your son, so your son knows he did not do well in the exams. What do you do? How do you handle this sudden attack on your dignity? I will tell you what Silfano did. He rebelled.

In the part of the country where I come from, there are squirrels. They live in holes. They do not make holes of their own, but live in holes made by certain ants. If they sense danger, they dash to the hole and disappear. If their hole is in or near your farm you are in trouble. They feed on sprouting (germinating) crops. Once inside the hole you cannot get them out unless you have a technique to do so. The best technique is to smoke them out. You light a fire at the entrance of the hole and fan the smoke into it. The squirrels would come out eventually. The more the smoke the faster the little beast comes out.

That's what Silfano did. He increased the volume and intensity of smoke on the Ojuodhi leadership spiritually and secularly. The man encouraged his people to take their children to schools in towns, particularly Kisumu, where his brother-in-law, Padre Reuben Omulo, was the head teacher. Ironically Reuben was also from Ojuodhi, but did not agree with his people on persecution of Jo-Umani. This way a few of his people acquired valuable education; otherwise it was a total educational curfew for them in Gem.

It was after the establishment of the Seventh-day Adventist schools that his people started learning in earnest, as the floodgates of education were finally opened. Almost all school-age children, boys and girls, went to school. The transformation was thorough and the impact immediate. People started reaping the benefits immediately, with the growing realization that the youth of today were the leaders of tomorrow. Those post-emancipation youths have indeed become the leaders in our country today.

But I'm getting ahead of myself.

When it became obvious that Silfano could not make use of his training, his only fault being that he was Ja-Umani and the schools and churches started by the Anglican Church were headed by Kagola people, he decided to raise the issue with Padre Nyende.

The padre said, "If you want to teach you must find a school for your own people where you can go and teach them foolishness."

Silfano took this with a positive attitude. A person's attitude can be a powerful tool indeed. To some, their attitude finds opportunity in every difficulty; others find difficulty in every opportunity. Some climb obstacles with a positive attitude while others fail because of a negative attitude. Silfano adopted a positive attitude to this scorn and took it in his stride.

But just what was Padre Nyende communicating to Silfano?

Let me say this. The statement was not only discriminatory; it was tribal, ethnic, unethical and deeply unchristian. But beyond that he considered Silfano's training bogus. He did not recognize the certificate Silfano had obtained from the only institution set up by the Anglican Church to train its teachers and clergy. Whatever the reason, the padre's unfortunate statement fired up the wrath of the Ojwando people. Silfano decided he had what it took to lead his people out of this misery. He was going to fight.

The struggle

If God is for us, who can be against us? He who did not spare His own son, but gave him up for us all – how will he not also, along with him, graciously give us all things? Rom 8:31-32 (NIV)

After Kenya was declared a British colony in 1920, the British organized the legal system to conform to their own. A Tribunal was the court of the first instance and dealt mainly with civil, divorce and land claims. Silfano, having so unfairly failed to join the profession of his calling, was appointed a member of a Tribunal by the British and was stationed at Ramula, in Gem, Central Kavirondo.

The Tribunal was the forerunner of African courts, which became courts of first instance, appeals from which went to Resident Magistrate courts. African courts would later be disbanded and replaced by District Magistrate courts, which would deal with all cases of civil and criminal nature in the first instance.

The British valued education so much that they could not allow Silfano, one of the few with education, to do nothing. The Anglican Church and the government were like one thing during those days. You could not differentiate one from the other.

The church, having denied Silfano and Andrea the opportunity to teach or preach, the government's hands were tied. They could not force the church to hire these two men. But they also knew that the Ojwando people, particularly Jo-Umani, would be furious and would make a lot of noise. So they appointed Silfano a member of the Tribunal and posted him to Ramula, in Gem Location. He was the first Ja-Umani to hold such a post, the second being Justo Wamboga Ofula, and lately Justice Fred Andago Ochieng, a Judge of the High Court of Kenya.

Silfano served in Ramula in 1936 and part of 1937 and rose in rank to become the Tribunal's chairman. While he was away, engaged in the administration of justice, the agitation machinery, which he had organized and put in place went into full gear. No force on earth was going to stop it. Silfano acquired the legal knowledge to enable him perform the work God had called him to accomplish. He learnt to arbitrate disputes with fairness, always being guarded and guided by God. He learned to be firm, and in his demeanor exhibited virtues of a true Christian.

A true CHRISTIAN is:

Caring

Happy

Respectable

Industrious

Sincere

Tolerant

Inspiring

Amiable

Neighborly

Silfano had all these virtues. He prayed endlessly for God's blessings, not for himself, because he was not selfish, but for the oppressed everywhere. He prayed to God to forgive the church and the administrators who were out to decimate whole tribes in Gem. He prayed for their forgiveness because they did not know what they were doing.

They rejoiced in the suffering of other people without realizing that God always sided with the underdog who genuinely believed in Him. No, they did not know that they were putting spells and

The struggle

curses on their children, grandchildren and the grandchildren of their children. They failed to realize there were generational curses people brought upon themselves; and that the evils they did to others would one day return to haunt them. They should have heeded the words of two proverbs. Here is the first: *A fault confessed is half redressed.* And the second: *Even an ant may hurt an elephant.* How true. The point is, these folks had acquired the power of an elephant and had expected no trouble at all from an ant. But future events would prove them dead wrong. Two things happened that accelerated the emancipation of the oppressed in Gem. Let me get right to them.

The oppressors tightened the noose they had placed round the neck of the oppressed. Things went from bad to worse. Whereas they had been going around gathering oppressed people for manual labour, this time they got physical. They whipped people who resisted and didn't care whether one was sick or not. They became brutes. Even women were not spared.

There was the ugly and sacrilegious incident of 1937, when goons and hoodlums attacked Ojwando people as they were having their Sunday worship in church. This was forgiven but not forgotten. I hope God forgave them too!

One of the direct consequences of denying Silfano and Andrea teaching and preaching jobs was seen and felt in the church. Tension was high in the Malanga Anglican Church, where Ojwando people, particularly Jo-Umani and Kagola people, fellowshipped. There was mistrust between them; and the intrigues of the Kagola people didn't help. The padre in charge, instead of being a pacifier and peacemaker, stoked the fires. Instead of being neutral, he sided with his people because they did his bidding. They wanted the church for themselves. They did not want to share even Christ with *mwache* (referring to the Ojwando people).

The head of the Anglican Church at the time was Archdeacon Owen, whose residence and offices were in Ng'iya, in Alego. Owen was an intelligent, hardworking, impartial and fair administrator. He doubled up as the African representative in the Legislative Council of Kenya. His interest and brief was to maintain peace and convert souls to Christ in the Kavirondo area. Like other British administrators of the time, he never took sides in local politics. Ojwando people made several representations to him, both on church and governance related issues, but he didn't appear engaged. I believe he was also aware of the debarment of Silfano and Andrea, but did not do anything.

But when the matter of disunity and mutual suspicion threatened to break up the church and scatter the flock, he had to do something. He summoned Padre Simion Nyende for interrogation. He must have visited with Chief Ogada Odera as well, because Chief Ogada and Padre Nyende worked in cahoots. As things got clearer, Owen was finally ready to take action. He summoned a meeting of the Rural Deanery. Silfano got wind of this and attended. By Solomonic wisdom, Archdeacon Owen decided that resolution of this matter rested on the introduction of two Sunday services—one for Ojwando people, the other for Kagola people. Ojwando people were to attend the morning service and Ojuodhi people the afternoon service. That arrangement brought peace in the church and members continued to pray as per the Archdeacon's directive.

But this did not last long. Ojuodhi people didn't like it. They wanted a full cake. They wanted exclusion and expulsion of Ojwando members from the church. They became hostile, aggressive and more and more antagonistic to, and resentful of, Ojwando members of the church. When tension persisted and

The struggle

even intensified, Silfano went to the Archdeacon, but nothing was done. Other than Malanga, there were nine other Anglican churches. They were: Lundha, Maliera, Muhaka, Luanda, Regea, Umina, Nyamninia, Gogo and Sirembe. God had done wonders in the area of evangelization. His Word spread fast among the Kavirondo people. The Roman Catholics were not left behind. Once they started providing education, teaching their members how to read and write, they converted many too. But Chief Ogada, who was the reigning chief, did not like them too.

It was Silfano's cousin, a man by the name Joseph Okola, who brought Roman Catholic in Gem, Mutumbu. He started teaching people, including kids, Catholic doctrines. One day the chief came with his *askaris* (police), got hold of him, beat him up thoroughly, tied him on the trunk of a tree and left him there to die. The children did not escape the whip either. They were chased, caught and whipped. Their only mistake was that they were Umani kids being taught Catechism by Ja-Umani. Anything Umani was anathema to Chief Ogada. The Anglican Church padre in charge of Gem joined him in this. They wanted to put a seal on the spiritual growth of the people. But Okola defied the might of the chief and the intrigues of the Anglican Church padre and continued with his crusade. There was no stopping him.

***

In 1956 a primary school was started where Okola was beaten. This school grew and surprised friend and foe when it developed into a fully-fledged girl's high school. Today it caters for everybody; Ojuodhi children included, but sits on Silfano's people's ancestral land. This land was set apart for public use by our forefathers in their foresight. The church moved its building from the school compound and constructed it across the road, opposite the school. Today it caters for the entire location, but it is a pale shadow of Seventh-day Adventist membership in the area. There is no home in the area where inhabitants don't go to church. With the exception of a couple of struggling Islamists, the entire population in Gem, especially North Gem, is Christian albeit of different denominations.

6

SACRILEGE

For you are all sons of God through faith in Christ Jesus. For as many of you as were baptized in to Christ have put on Christ. There is neither Jew nor Greek, there is neither slave nor free, there is neither male nor female; for you are all one in Christ Jesus. And if you are Christ's, then you are Abraham's seed, and heirs according to the promise. Gal 3:2629 (NKJV)

On the 28th of March 1937, Ojuodhi people desecrated the church. It was a morning like any other. Ojwando church members had prepared their children for the Sunday morning service as per Archdeacon Owen's directive. Silfano Ayayo was not among those who had prepared to go to Malanga Church that morning because he was away, probably at his workstation. Every Ojwando person who had embraced the Lord—man, woman and child—was to attend church service. If Silfano were there, he would have led this service. But today someone else was going to lead the service.

Philip Obonyo was there, and so were Festo Oyolo, Nickolao Wanyanga, Barnabas Ndula, Simion Ambayo, Elijah Okech and many others. Young people, women and children were in this congregation to fellowship and praise the Lord. The congregation was visibly elated. Only a few months before they did not have a free atmosphere to worship. Now they did.

Triumph Through Faith

So this Sunday, like previous ones, they had a whole Sunday morning preserved for just them. They probably wanted to prove their numerical strength as well. They carried their tithes and offerings for the Lord. They were in church, but in their hearts they felt as if they were heaven-bound. Little did they know that hired hooligans would ruin their day. The service started and went on as planned. Tithes and offerings were collected. People sang hymns in praise of God. Children were taught from the Gospels. The church was full; some new members were in the congregation. Their names were quickly recorded for placement in the baptismal class.

Then, without the slightest warning, hell broke loose. Strong Kagola men emerged from behind the thickets around the church armed with walking sticks (*bakora*) and leather whips made from the hide of hippopotamus, which were the weapons of choice at the time. They descended on the people inside the church and beat them up. Then huge men, ensuring nobody escaped, blocked the two exits. They beat up men, women and children who were armed only with Bibles. At first there was yelling and crying from women and children, but this suddenly stopped when the men decided to defend themselves and their women and children. They confronted their assailants on a one on one combat. Strong women like Rosa Okuot Nyar Midenge joined the fight to help their men. The scene was chaotic. After a couple of minutes, the men and women in the congregation repulsed the ugly aggressors. Several people were injured, men, women and children. There were injuries too on the bouncers and musclemen of the Kagola clan. Chairs, pews and tables were broken. Torn pages of Bibles littered the floor. Some people used Bibles as a weapon or armor. The tithes and offerings went missing. And although the aggressors were pushed out of the church building, skirmishes continued in the church compound.

Sacrilege

The injured in the congregation were later rushed to Malanga Dispensary. The injured among Kagola assailants did not go to Malanga Dispensary for fear of being lynched by Jo-Umani.

Word of this incident spread like bush fire among the Ojwando people. Folks were outraged by this unprovoked barbarism. They could not suppress their anger and indignation. People gathered in clusters to discuss the incident. Many asserted that the Anglican Church was not the only church and that if the Kagola clan wanted them out they were ready to move elsewhere. Others suggested they should have a different building, but continue to be Anglicans. One thing, however, was clear—they were not going back to Malanga Anglican Church for worship. They attended subsequent Sunday services under a huge tree in front of Petro Ongwen's home. It was from this point onward that people rallied behind Silfano to a man. He assumed the leadership gladly and never looked back. He became the leader of Jo-Umani and all Ojwando people.

Later people learned that this heinous and barbaric act had been hatched and planned by the Chief and the Padre. Their aim was to chase Ojwando people from the church. They were not content with denying the people their God-given right to education; they were not content to deny the trained teachers schools to teach in; and were not content to deny their trained clergy churches to minister in—they were intent on denying the people spiritual life, their Christ, their God, and their salvation. But God, the living God, was not going to allow this to happen. He had come in time to stop this madness!

But I'm getting ahead of myself.

On getting news of desecration of the church, Silfano immediately protested to Archdeacon Owen. This time the Archdeacon took prompt action, after all this was not just a spiritual crime; it was also battery and assault, some of which amounted to grievous bodily harm. These were offences against the laws of the land, which Archdeacon Owen had the mandate to enforce. He called members of the Rural Deanery once again. This time the Deanery met at Lundha Church. The Rural Deanery members did not only reprimand and warn Padre Nyende of dire consequences if he continued the hate and annihilation campaign against Ojwando people, which he'd carried on along with Chief Ogada, but suspended the padre and stopped him from ministering to Ojwando people. The ten churches were also divided between the Ojwando and Ojuodhi people as follows: Malanga, Maliera, Lundha, Muhaka and Luanda for Ojwando, and Regea, Umina, Gogo, Sirembe and Nyamninia for Ojuodhi. Padre Nyende continued to minister in Ojuodhi churches while the Ojwando churches came under the leadership of Silfano. Ojwando church members were directed to take their babies to Padre Barnabas Weche, of Namasoli Anglican Church, for dedication and baptism, since Silfano had not been ordained a padre yet. This arrangement continued until a padre who could work with *Mwache* was identified and posted to minister to them. But since Ojwando people were not comfortable with their membership in the Anglican Church, God had other plans for them.

Silfano, by hindsight, came to realize that for his people to progress, they had to have power, which was concentrated in three institutions. In the spiritual world, power was in the hands of the church and her clergy. In the secular world, it was in the hands of the administrators, those who governed and maintained law and order. This is what obtained at that time. He realized that the Ojwando people had to have a church they could use as a vehicle to educate their children. Churches at that time were the only credible institutions that had manpower, finance and organizational capability to run schools. They

Sacrilege

needed clergy, church-trained ministers and other personnel who could man the churches. And they had to have teachers to teach in the new schools. In this regard, they had to have access to training institutions, which were also run by the churches. Ojwando people had none of the above except two teachers and two clergy in Silfano and Andrea.

If you want to teach, you must find a school for your own people, where you can go and teach them foolishness.

Those words echoed in Silfano's mind with the clarity of roaring thunder. He knew he had to accept the challenge from the padre and do something for his people. He knew there would be hard times ahead for him and the people, but they had to trudge right ahead. He knew the struggle wasn't going to be a bed of roses, but they had to soldier on. He knew that his life was in danger and would continue to be in danger, but he had to focus on the struggle. Each step along the way he focused on Jesus and the cross. He understood that Jesus died for the salvation of *all* mankind—Ojwando people included.

He knew that Christ would protect him if he had faith in Him. He thus had nothing to fear. But because God helps those who help themselves, he had to take precaution for his safety and the safety of his family. A 24-hour security watch was arranged and put in place for this purpose. And finally the stage was set for an epic battle.

Those words emboldened Silfano's resolve and encouraged him to establish Maliera Sector School in 1938, the only Private Sector School at the time.

7

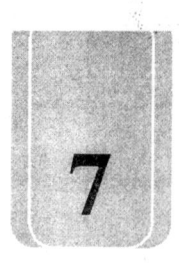

RESCUED BY THE SEVENTH-DAY ADVENTIST CHURCH

But seek first the kingdom of God and his righteousness, and all these things shall be added to you. Matthew 6:33 (NKJV)

Muscular men were not the only people at *Bungu* during the night to watch over the safety of the leader. Elders felt that if Silfano were to be harmed by anybody that person would kill them before he could reach him. They were ready to die for him.

These elders were Musa Adongo, Mathayo Oduma, Nickolao Wanyanga, Wilson Mbola, Isaka Otieno and others. They were devoted Christians whose only concern was the spiritual and secular welfare of their people. They were in *Bungu* every night to beef up security and to pray to the Almighty to guide them by opening ways for them and their children. They wanted a church. They wanted a school to which their kids could go after STD 3. They needed secular power to enable them to participate in the governance of their people. They had a lot to ask of their Creator. What better place to pray and meditate than the serene atmosphere of *Bungu,* where security was guaranteed? These meetings were held nightly and the group of elders participating was named Kokelo. The prayers went on for weeks, until they decided to fast as they prayed, for as long as it would take God to answer their prayers. They would never give up.

One day, after they had prayed and fasted a whole day and were now resting on their seats, they fell asleep. Three elders—Musa Adongo, Mathayo Oduma and Silfano—had a simultaneous vision in their dream. In the dream, they were directed to read Isaiah 66:22-23. The first one to wake up woke up the others to narrate to them what he had seen in the dream. As the other two woke up, they said they too had a vision. They sought to know what each elder had seen in the dream. Was it similar?

Silfano narrated his dream first. He said, "As I was sleeping, a Bible text was revealed to me."

"Interesting," one of the other two said. "I've just had a similar experience!"

"And me too," the third said.

On that note each of the three was given a piece of paper to write the text. Lo and behold, the text was the same. It was Isaiah 66:22-23. They fetched their Bibles and read. It said:

"As the new heavens and the new earth that I make will endure before me," declares the LORD, "so will your name and descendants endure. V23 From one New Moon to another and from one Sabbath to another, all mankind will come and bow down before me," says the LORD. (NIV)

The elders were perplexed. It was incredible. How could three people have the same dream simultaneously? Their opinion was irrespective of what this scripture meant, it must have come from God. God had answered their vigil, prayers and fasting, although they did not understand one word from what the scripture said. They knew every word except Sabbath. They had not heard this word before.

The Anglican priests who taught them the Bible did not mention this word. They decided to seek the meaning of this word from Archdeacon Owen. They sent a delegation, led by Silfano, which met the Archdeacon for interpretation. The Archdeacon did not give them the interpretation. Either he did not know what to tell them or he knew but declined to talk. He, instead, gave them a letter and directed them to go to his brother missionary in Gendia, South Kavirondo, where there was a Christian church worshipping on Sabbath. Thus a delegation composed of Silfano as the leader, Mathayo Oduma, Fanuel Odhiambo, Musa Adongo, Elsham Odera and Zakayo Wasiembi, set off for Gendia in August 1939. The issue was the Sabbath!

They arrived during the camp meeting. A camp meeting is one of the several annual events in the Seventh-day Adventist yearly calendar. Adherents camp out a whole week fellowshipping, worshipping and praising God. It was quite significant that the delegation arrived in Gendia when the camp meeting was on. It gave them the opportunity to observe Seventh-day Adventists at their best. They listened to the preachers, the testimonies and songs of praise. They interacted with seasoned pastors, trained evangelists, elders and laity. They watched children's programs and Sabbath school services. They were there for one week.

Later, the delegation stayed in Gendia as guests of the church, learning about the Sabbath and other fundamental church beliefs. They saw a big disparity in the attitude of these Gendia Christians and the Christians they had been used to back home. The Gendia Christians were not only welcoming, but their faces radiated love and affection. At each home they visited, and

Rescued by the Seventh-day Adventist Church

these were several, the welcome was warm and cheerful. They talked to the church leadership, led by Pastor Thomas, about the reason for their visit and agreed on all matters at hand. The church leaders agreed to come to Central Kavirondo for a crusade, which they believed would produce the seeds to plant a Seventh-day Adventist church there. That was the plan. The delegation returned home elated and exuded rare confidence. They had gone for an explanation of what *Sabbath* meant, but did not only find an explanation they also found a church!

It's a fascinating story, but let me back up a little. Before leaving for Gendia the people had wanted separation from the Ojuodhi clans. They did not want to mix with them in church any more. The Gendia visit gave them more than they asked for—a different church, different doctrines and a different day of worship. They returned convinced that God had answered their prayers, night vigils and fasting. *The church, which observed the Sabbath day, was the church they were going to lead their flock to.* This church would give them a complete break from the Anglicans and the Catholics. They would go from worshiping on Sunday to worshiping on Saturday.

On return, the delegation reported back to the people who sent them, who upon hearing the news were equally ecstatic. So on the sixteenth day of December 1939, Pastor Thomas, Pastor Isaac Okeyo, Pastor Joshua Ouma and Evangelist Joshua Rume came to Central Kavirondo and conducted a prayer meeting at Kodiaga, in what is now North Gem. A mammoth crowd attended it. People marveled at the sheer number of people in attendance. A religious meeting had never attracted such a large gathering before. At the end of the crusade more than one thousand people were baptized into the Seventh-day Adventist Church. The Ojwando groups and all churches under Silfano crossed over and were baptized. Because of the huge number of converts, baptism took two days, because they were done through immersion in accordance with Seventh-day Adventist beliefs. It was a big and memorable occasion, a carnival of sorts, marked with songs of praises to God. Yes, the seeds were planted, but it was now upon the elders to tend and water the seeds so they would sprout, grow and bear fruit.

A couple of weeks later, at the request of the elders, the Adventist missionaries in Gendia sanctioned the installation of a Seventh-day Adventist administration in all the five Anglican churches that were under the control of Silfano: Malanga, Maliera, Lundha, Muhaka and Luanda. Pastor Joshua Ouma was the first posting from Gendia. He came to nurse and nurture the young churches, to place them on a firm pedestal—an onerous but honorable task indeed. This pastor (Ouma), with the help of Silfano and other stalwarts of the struggle, discharged this responsibility with distinction. The churches flourished and helped establish other churches in the region and beyond. Never in the history of Adventism had so many people been won for Christ and baptized in a single crusade, except of course at the Pentecost, where three thousand people were baptized (Acts 2:41). Never had so many people's salvation hinged on so few. A hero, a school and now a church, working with and through the Almighty God, broke the chain of bondage and released a people from the yoke of oppression. So finally, with the establishment of the Maliera Sector School, their children's education was guaranteed. The Seventh-day Adventist Church met their second triangle of needs—the spiritual. They were now left with the battle in the secular field, where people were still barred from participating in governance. Silfano would later lead the fight for governance and win. But we'll come to that later. All the five churches were coordinated from *Bungu*—Silfano's home. The pastors who were posted to Central Kavirondo stayed with Silfano at his *Bungu* home.

The following is a list of the pastors who worked at Maliera Mission Station from 1939 to 2012:

NO.	LICENCED AND ORDAINED PASTORS
1.	Joshua Ouma
2.	Isaac Okeyo
3.	Thadayo Nyan'ganga
4.	Israel Okoth
5.	Ezekiel Rewe
6.	Luka Amayo
7.	Shelemiah Nyatawa
8.	Christopher Odero
9.	Solomon Okoye
10.	Mathayo Wandiga
11.	Nicholao Opiyo
12.	Ephrahim Odero
13.	Mordekayi Awuor
14.	Fredrick Awuor
15.	James Opere
16.	Ephrahim Odero
17.	Daniel Oyugi
18.	Shadrack Wahonya
19.	Sospeter Amollo

NO.	LICENCED AND ORDAINED PASTORS
20.	Noah Adero
21.	Josephat Inyangala
22.	David Augo
23.	Boaz Otuoma
24.	Daniel Sidho
25.	Albert Otieno
26.	Meshack Ogembo
27.	Isaiah Dete
28.	Hezron Sande
29.	John Olongo
30.	Joash Ooko
31.	Justus Abondo

The Adventist Church was by now firmly established in Central Kavirondo, but was this the only effort to introduce Adventism into the region? No, it wasn't. In 1927 Evangelist Joshua Rume came and preached to people and established a Seventh-day Adventist Church in Musembe, in what is now known as North Gem Location. He ministered there for a while, but had to cut short his work to return to his family, which he had left behind in South Kavirondo—at a place known these days as Kandiege, in Rachuonyo District.

The church Rume established at Musembe collapsed in his absence because he had not left it in the hands of a strong person. But he returned in 1933 to Musembe, where as a result of his preaching, a Seventh-day Adventist Church was once

Rescued by the Seventh-day Adventist Church

again established. When he returned to his home the church disintegrated again and members abandoned it. To cut this short, the church in Musembe would later get going again and became established under the leadership of future leaders of the rapidly growing Adventist Church.

***

Silfano's efforts in bringing Adventism to Central Kavirondo were the third attempt; others had failed. This third effort succeeded beyond measure, courtesy of God's grace upon Silfano and his organizational ability. And by then Silfano's greatness had started being manifest. Great people are sometimes ordinary people with an extraordinary amount of determination. That was Silfano. He had an extraordinary amount of determination and drive, which he used to work for the emancipation of his people. That his greatness was felt only around Gem and church mission posts in Nyanza should never diminish his stature as one of Kenya and Adventism's most illustrious sons. Note also that at around the same time the Adventist church was in Gem, it was also established in Nyalgunga in Alego and Naya in Uyoma.

From Maliera, Adventism spread to Central Kavirondo (the present-day Kisumu and Siaya counties) and North Kavirondo (the present-day Kakamega, Bungoma, Busia and Vihiga counties). Central Kavirondo has one field: Central Nyanza Field established in 1990. At inception, it comprised Butere, Siaya, Busia, Kisumu, Nyando and Bondo districts. Later Busia and Butere churches, except a few which decided to remain, were hived off and placed under Western Kenya Conference. Its first Executive Director was Pastor Joseph Okello. It became Central Nyanza Conference in 2015.

Triumph Through Faith

Maliera Seventh-day Adventist Sector School

Knowledge is horizontal, Wisdom is vertical it comes down from above. Billy Graham

After Adventism had been established and had taken root, Silfano asked the missionaries in Gendia to take over the Maliera Sector School. If they accepted, it was going to have three significant advantages to the parents, the teachers, the pupils and Silfano himself. Parents were going to get relief in contributing money for teachers' salaries. Teachers were going to have a secure source of income. Pupils were going to have an outlet after STD 3 in Kamagambo Adventist School, which had been started by the Adventists to cater for pupils going to STD 4. And for Silfano, this was going to be a big relief, as it would remove the burden of ensuring teachers were paid and necessary teaching aids like chalk, slates and graphite pens availed to the pupils. He was also going to be relieved of administrative chores, which he was performing as owner of the project.

On receiving the request, the missionaries accepted gladly and took over full responsibility of running the school. The name changed to Maliera Seventh-day Adventist Sector School. This was the 1940 school year.

In 1946, Maliera Seventh-day Adventist Sector School became Maliera Seventh-day Adventist Primary School. The school progressed steadily, producing competent graduates who proceeded to deploy into strategic positions in the country. In 1957, the Kenya Colonial Government allowed the Seventh-day Adventists to establish Intermediate classes in the Maliera Seventh-day Adventist Primary School. Thus STD 5 and STD 6 were started simultaneously and the first Kenya African Preliminary Examination (KAPE) was done in 1959. It was a magical moment. Later, as a result of the government's change in policy, all primary and intermediate schools were brought

Rescued by the Seventh-day Adventist Church

under district education boards, and Maliera, along with other church-run primary and intermediate schools, were taken over. Churches, however, retained their sponsorship roles and Maliera continued to be sponsored by the Seventh-day Adventists.

***

In 1968, Maliera Mixed Day Secondary School was started. This was done under the care of the Seventh-day Adventist Church, following the recommendations of a team of government inspectors, which visited the School on 17th December 1967. The secondary school, in spite of teething problems, registered steady progress, which was eventually recognized by the government; which later accorded it self-help status in 1971. Then in 1981 the government took over maintenance of the school.

From its very humble beginning, Maliera progressed and became a crucial school, competing with the best schools in Nyanza Province and beyond in academic excellence. It provided a springboard for higher learning for all the children of Kenya. The success of Maliera School brought Ojwando people at par with their oppressors academically. It did not only serve the purpose for which it was established, it also served as a tool in the struggle for emancipation of Ojwando people. It leveled the playing field. The school being his brainchild, Silfano never ceased to pray for its growth and stability. Indeed, that the school is in its present form and outlook is clear evidence of a prayer answered. Maliera shall continue to rise! (For a detailed history of Maliera School see *The History of Maliera School*, a book by this author.)

Triumph Through Faith

As a result of Silfano's effort of bringing the Seventh Day Adventist Church to Central Nyanza the following schools and churches were established:-

CHURCHES STARTED:

Maliera (main)	Rawalo	Olengo
Malanga	Rabuor	Bar Dimba
Muhaka	Bar Sauri	Nyangoma
Luanda	Yala Township	Nyadeha
Lundha	Tie Yath	Sinaga
Musembe	Sarika	Siala Kaduol
Murumba	Wagai	Ulamba
Nyanya	Madiri	Masene
	Masogo	Uholo
Ngiya Sirembe Nyapiedho	Nyandhondho Sega	Magoya Huluga
	Jera	Muhanda
Maliera Central	Ugunja	Funyula
Ndere	Ramula	Kambare
Sidindi	Bar Owan'g	Nyamninia
Regea/Kisendo	Ukwala	Anyiko
Magunda	Busia	Marenyo
New Life	Ogero	Sinaga

SCHOOLS ESTABLISHED

Maliera

Luanda

Rescued by the Seventh-day Adventist Church

Muhaka
Kamnara
Naya
Sanda
Makasembo
Thur Gem
Nyalgunga
Ochiewa
Cherwa
Olembo
Musembe
Bar Sauri
Wang'arot

8

EMIGRATION

Get out of your country, from your family and from your father's house, to a land that I will show you. Gen 12:1 (NKJV)

Like most of his peers, Silfano was baptized into the Seventh-day Adventist faith on the 17th day of December 1939. This baptism was special. It was the first time people here saw baptism by immersion and it was unique because of the number of people who were baptized. His wife, Asenath, was among the women baptized. After his baptism, he went into overdrive in his efforts to consolidate Adventism in the region. He helped the community build proper structures for its churches.

Corrugated iron sheets, commonly used on roofing houses in rural areas in Western Kenya, were not available then, so *olenge* (thin long stems of an African grass), which was the best roofing stuff available and the preserve of the rich, was used in roofing the churches. It was hard to come by *olenge* and it was found only in areas that were not populated. All Adventist churches

Emigration

constructed at the time used this roofing stuff. The roofing done by experts (they were quite few) would last fifty years.

Silfano moved from place to place looking into the construction of these church buildings and preaching and evangelizing. He did the evangelism work as a church elder since he had not been ordained as a minister yet. The Anglicans had trained him, but their doctrines and practices were completely different from those of the Seventh-day Adventists. He could not be ordained as a minister unless he was first trained as a minister in the Adventist faith.

In 1941, he enrolled at the Kamagambo Training College for a two-year pastoral training course. After this training, he was posted to Nyalgunga Seventh-day Adventist Church, in Alego, in 1943. He then was subjected to unusual transfers. He was posted to Alego, from Gem, then to South Nyanza, where he worked at different places, including Kadem, Karungu, Mihuru, Wire and many other places.

When he was transferred to South Nyanza, he started experiencing traveling problems as he had to come back occasionally to see his family. He agonized a lot and finally decided to seek God's guidance on this. He had two options at the time. He could ask church authorities to transfer him back to Central Nyanza or he could turn his back completely on Central Nyanza and let God lead him wherever He wanted.

The former option, however, was riddled with danger. First, there was the fear that he could be assassinated by his foes. The second was the welfare of his children. He wanted his children to grow up under his watchful eye and to have a good education. He wanted them to raise good families and be prosperous. Third, as he was out there on God's calling, which had been his goal since his youth, he wanted to put both his soul and mind into it. Fourth, his home had become a mission station; moving would displace the mission. Without alternative land to build a mission station, the work would collapse. Members of the LNC in the area, a body whose responsibility was to identify and allocate land to churches and schools, had vowed never to give any land to the Adventists—Ojwando people. That's when he remembered what God told Abraham:

Leave your country, your people and your father's household and go to the land I will show you. Gen 12:1 (NIV)

And he remembered another significant spiritual text:

If God is for us, who can be against us? Roman 8:31 (NKJV)

He understood that if God did it for Abraham, He could do it for him. He also remembered an old adage which says, "The distance between one and salvation is the distance between his knee and the ground." He knelt and prayed that God would give him direction. God directed him to leave Gem, his father's household, his friends, his peers and the comrades on whose side he had fought many battles. Like Abraham, he left his home not knowing where he would go and what the future held for him. But the time had come!

So in 1944, he relocated. He got part of his family out of *Bungu* and took them to South Nyanza. The first group comprised himself, his wife Asenath, and his children—ABC Ochola Ayayo, Beldina Akeyo and Amos Ochieng Ayayo who was still a toddler. Sipora Akumu, Nahor Odhiambo, Hellen Omolo and Christine Adhiambo followed them later. Tobias Otieno Ayayo, Prisca Odero and Herina Okuom were left at *Bungu* to look after the home. In 1945, though, Tobias Otieno Ayayo and Prisca Odero joined the first group in South Nyanza. Then the last group of Herina Okuom and Dina Omolo completed the family's migration.

Emigration

In 1946, Pastor Silfano built his first home in South Nyanza, at a place called Nyandago. Nyandago was a wilderness then. He stayed with his household in this area for four years, visiting them often from his work station. But in 1949, an unusual thing happened: the Nyandago home was hit by a thunderbolt and every structure and whatever was therein perished in the ensuing fire. Pastor Silfano was back to square one. All his earthly belongings perished. The only consolation was— none of his family members got hurt.

Traditionalists visited the tragic scene and talked. *A homestead built in the middle of nowhere struck by lightning? Was it normal?* These guys had a field day speculating on the cause of the tragedy. To them, the ancestors did not want the homestead there because it disturbed the peace of the dead. Some of the friends might have said, *"I told you that place is not desolate for nothing!"*

But Pastor Silfano was calm and composed. It did not worry him that he had lost his entire harvest. It didn't worry him that he had lost his livestock, furniture, clothes, chickens and everything. He was calm. He cast his eyes to the cross and saw the Lord and remembered his words in Matthew 6:26:

Look at the birds of the air; they do not sow or reap or store away in barns, and yet your heavenly Father feeds them. Are you not much more valuable than they? (NIV)

Pastor Silfano was definitely much more valuable than the birds and he knew his God and savior was not about to abandon him. He knew God would provide for his every need and would replenish what he had lost. While still pondering his next move, his mind wandered to 2 Corinthians 9:8:

"And God is able to make all grace abound to you, so that in all things at all times, having all that you need, you will abound in every good work. (NIV)

Triumph Through Faith

The Lord listened to his cry and led His servant to a different location—where because of his magnanimity, and out of love for his father's family and his cousins—he invited his brother, Japheth Wandago, in 1951, to join him in Kanyamkago, in Migori, where he had moved and established a home in 1950. He lived in this home for the rest of his life. Japheth came with his wife, Ludia Nyawire, and son, Kepha Owino. They were later joined by their first born son, Christopher Odongo. Pastor Silfano arranged and settled them on the land next to his.

In 1951, he invited his nephew, Gad Mayienga Ogola, who came and stayed with him while going to school at Nyamome. This nephew completed his education at Sigalagala, with Pastor Silfano providing his fees and needs. Later his cousin Fanuel Odhiambo and nephews Nehemiah Onyango and Odit Obonyo completed the list of immigrants. Surprisingly, his brother, Japheth Wandago, like his elder brother, Nickodemo Ogola, refused to embrace the Seventh-day Adventist faith and remained Anglicans.

In 1959, his beloved wife Asenath Ngalo died. This was a big blow to the family. It came so unexpectedly and caught the entire family off-guard. She had stayed in her new home for only nine years. Most of her children were not in high school yet. Pastor Tobias Otieno Ayayo, ABC Ochola Ayayo and Beldina were the only adult children at the time. Pastor Silfano was devastated but took solace in the Lord. He knew that since he was in the heaven-bound team God would one day wipe away his tears. He found consolation in the comforting words of Revelation 21:4:

"...*And God will wipe away every tear from their eyes; there shall be no more death, nor sorrow, nor crying. There shall be no more pain, for the former things have passed away.*" (NKJV)

Emigration

Consoling words indeed! Eventually he overcame his grief and continued in his path of uprightness, and with God's help saw all his remaining children through school. But I think I'm getting far down the stream. It's important to capture the way Mama's death affected the pastor and the children—and even other folks around them. Let me wear their shoes for a moment.

Pastor Silfano lost an aide, a companion and a comforter. He lost a friend that had stood by him in sorrow and in happiness. He lost an invisible general who had fought throughout the emancipation war. He lost a homemaker who was the envy of many. He lost a mother whose love, care and affection for her children was unrivaled. He lost a lover whose love to him was boundless. He was going to miss the help, companionship and comfort, which was the hallmark in his home. He was going to miss a comrade in arms and an excellent rearguard general. He was going to miss an advisor par excellence. He was going to miss friends who flocked to his home and were received by a disarming smile.

The children were not spared the anguish either. *Why did Mother go so early? Who is going to help Father look after us?* These were some of the questions on their minds. They were questions, which not even their father was able to answer. They grieved in their hearts and for a long time did not know what to do. Unlike their father, who was harsh and uncompromising, the mother was meek and tactful. They missed the good food. Asenath was an excellent cook; any food she touched was delicious. She belonged to the class of those mothers who had learned and perfected the art of traditional cooking. They could cook food without using oil or salt and still come out tasty and delicious. Mother loved and protected them with the zeal and gusto of a hen protecting her little ones. She never wanted them to be hurt or to suffer in any way. Now she was gone!

The church community was going to miss her too. She had been such a devout Christian, holding positions of leadership. She was loved and appreciated by the entire church fraternity. She was a member of the 3rd choir (*mony mar adek*) of the church. With her beautiful voice, she helped the choir grow from strength to strength and that made her be loved even more.

The village community would miss her as well. She had been discharging her social responsibilities with devotion. She was there for them in joy and in sorrow, in birth and in death. Her life had been a reflection of the life of Jesus Christ. She was a mirror through which people saw their shortcomings. Her life was the standard through which people measured their morality and uprightness. The gap left, as a result of her demise, was going to be hard to fill.

But the greatest burden remained the one left in the heart of Pastor Silfano. The wise words of Solomon, from which he had derived so much solace and hope, rang repeatedly in his mind. *He who finds a wife finds a good thing, and obtains favor from the LORD* (Proverbs 18:22). He was fired up by these words when he "dated" Asenath. He had felt lonely before he met and married her, leaving his parents and clinging to her, and now he was back to that loneliness. The gap left in his heart was going to be hard to fill indeed.

9

THE MINISTRY

Then I heard the voice of the Lord saying, "Whom shall I send? And who will go for us?" And I said, "Here am I. Send me!" Isaiah 6:8 (NIV)

After his ordination in 1945, Pastor Silfano continued his ministry work, under Gendia Mission Station, the forerunner of Kenya Lake Field, which later became Kenya Lake Conference. Kenya Lake Field, with headquarters in Kendu Bay (in present-day Homa Bay County), encompassed the administrative regions of Nyanza and Western Province, in the Republic of Kenya. Gendia Mission was the springboard from which other mission stations sprang.

SCHEDULE OF EARLY MISSION STATIONS AND WHEN THEY WERE ORGANIZED:

NO.	STATION	YEAR	WHO ORGANIZED
1.	Gendia	1906	Carscarllen/Bartlett/Yambo
2.	Kanyidoto	1911	Spark assisted by Mark Otieno

NO.	STATION	YEAR	WHO ORGANIZED
3.	Kamagambo	1912	Armstrong/Peter Oyier/E.R. Warland
4.	Nyanchwa	1912	Carscallen/Beavon/Jacob Olwa
5.	Wire	1912	Carscallen/J.D. Baker
6.	Ranen	1944	T. F. Duke/J.N. Smuts
7.	Maliera	1940	Pastor Joshua Ouma/Silfano Ayayo
8.	Rusinga	1912	Pastor Watson/Daniel Onyango

The establishment of Kamagambo Mission Station paved the way for the organization of Kamagambo Training College, where all Seventh-day Adventists wishing to take up preaching, as a calling, were trained. Teachers training followed closely, with secondary and primary schools being late additions. This writer had the privilege of learning at Kamagambo High School.

SCHEDULE OF EARLY MISSIONARIES AND WHERE THEY WORKED

NO.	STATION	NAMES
1.	GENDIA	Carscallen A. A. W. T. Barlett Maxwell S. C. Thomas F. H. Hyde Sparrow Mudaspark

The ministry

2.	KANYIDOTO	Spark Warland Armstrong W. W. Thomas Mathews Murdock Hyde
3.	KAMAGAMBO	E. R. Warland
4.	WIRE	J. D. Baker/E.B. Phillips
5.	KARURA	Pastor Jeremiah Oigo
6.	NYANCHWA	Pastor Beavon
7.	RANEN	T. F. Dukes/S.N. Smuts
8.	CHANGAMWE-MOMBASA	Pastor Wright Pastor Peter Risasi Pastor Israel Okoth
9.	BUGEMA – UGANDA	Pastor Mathayo Yugi Pastor Ezekiel Rewe
10.	UPARE – TANZANIA	Pastor Peter Risasi
11.	MALIERA	Pastor Joshua Ouma Silfano Ayayo

Alongside the white missionaries, there were African pioneer pastors who worked hard to spread the gospel, open mission stations and plant churches.

SCHEDULE OF PIONEER AFRICAN PASTORS AND EVANGELISTS AND THE STATIONS THEY WORKED IN

NO.	STATION	PASTOR
1.	Gendia	Isaac Okeyo
2.	Gendia	Paul Mboya
3.	Gendia	Joel Omer
4.	Wikondiek	Jacob Ochuodho
5.		Jeremiah Oigo
6.	Kanyamfwa	Jacob Olwa
7.		Elisha Olero
8.	Rusinga	Isaac Orwa
9.		Ezekiel Rewe
10.	Wire/Maliera	Joshua Ouma
11.		James Odero
12.	Kanyamwa	Elijah Dande
13.	Karungu	Barnaba Okeyo
14.	Kadem	Silfano Ayayo
15.	Kamagambo	Jairus Achola
16.	Kanyidoto	Clement Kotonya
17.		Paul Nyamweya
18.		Mathayo Ratemo
19.		Samson Ongaki
20.		Mariko Nyasinga

The ministry

NO.	STATION	PASTOR
21.		Yusuf Simba
22.		Jacob Atinda
23.		Samuel Amoke
24.		Luka Amayo
25.		Joshua Rume

In 1946, Pastor Hyde transferred Kanyidoto Mission Station to Ranen Hill, which remains its present site. Pastor T. F. Duke, who succeeded Pastor Hyde, took many years to build the station—finally completing it in 1960. Then on 28th December 1961, Ranen was established as a Field, detaching itself from Kenya Lake Field. This was the second expansion of missionary work after South Kenya Field—now South Kenya Conference and Nyamira Conference— had been established in 1912, covering Kisii and Kuria districts. Kenya Lake Field and Ranen Field were thus left to serve Nyanza Province and Western Province, in the Republic of Kenya.

***

Let me switch gears here a bit. Choices have consequences and Mijema's were no exception. His family was split down the middle when Adventism arrived on the scene. There were those who chose to remain in the Anglican Church initially, among them Silfano's elder stepbrother Nicodemus Ogola and his entire family. His stepsister Gladys Odiaga and her entire family, and his other stepbrother Japheth Wandago and his entire family. These were Mijema's first wife's family. A few members of these families, in the recent past, have joined the Adventist Church.

The entire Akumu family (Mijema's second family) moved to the Adventist Church when it was first introduced in Central Kavirondo. This included Pastor Silfano and his entire family, his stepbrother Dulo's entire family, and his sisters Herina Okuom and Keziah Nyangolo. These families received and continue to receive immense blessings from the Lord. If you watch the two phases of Mijema's family, you will see that indeed choices have consequences. Akumu's descendants chose to worship the Lord on the Sabbath and have continued to do so with dedication and commitment. Sample these:

Silfano Ayayo was a hero and ordained minister of the gospel in the Seventh-day Adventist Church. Pastor Silfano's eldest son, Tobias Otieno, was a teacher, an ordained minister of the Gospel and the Education Director of Ranen Field (Now Ranen Conference) at one time. He was born Anglican, converted to SDA, lived and retired in the faith. He is blessed!

SCHEDULE OF PASTOR SILFANO'S OTHER DESCENDANTS HOLDING POSITIONS IN THE S.D.A. CHURCH

NO.	NAME	POSITION	CHURCH
1.	Martin Omondi Otieno	Church Elder	Migori
2.	Zachary Ngalo Otieno	Church Elder	Baraton
3.	Steve Ochieng Otieno	Satellite Evangelism Director	Ranen SDA
4.	Paul Oluoch Otieno	Deacon	Lavington
5.	Jacob Okoth Ayayo	Church Elder	Got Kayayo
6.	Jeremiah Ochieng Ayayo	Sabbath School Superintendent	Kakamega Central

The ministry

7.	Roseline A. Ochieng	Pastor and Principal	Ranen SDA Sec School
8.	Sam Oyieke Ayayo	Preacher	Freelance
9.	Mama Esther Achieng Ayayo	Deaconess	Got Kayayo
10.	Rosebella Otieno Ayayo	Deaconess	Got Kayayo
11.	Mary Oyieke	Deaconess and church Secretary	Got Kayayo
12.	Asenath Ngalo Odongo	Deaconess New Life	Nairobi
13.	Christine Adhiambo	Deaconess, Ngere Church Treasurer	
14.	Suzzy Ngalo Otieno	Deaconess Baraton	
15.	Musa Oswago Ayayo	Choir Leader New Life Nairobi	
16.	Opondo Ayayo	Youth Leader	Got Kayayo
17.	Asenatha Wamalwa	Health Director	Siaya Central
18.	Nerea Amos Ochieng	Head Deaconess	Got Kayayo
19.	Edwina Atieno Ombado	Personal Ministry Secretary New Life-Nairobi	

20.	Beldinah Akeyo Ayayo	Widows Leader Kalwal Kalwal SDA Station VOP Leader	
21.	James Ayodo Otieno	Medical Missionary Movement International team member	Georgia Cumberland Conference of SDA
22.	Dorcas Ayodo	Executive Committee Member Medical Missionary Movement International and Secretary African Chapter.	Georgia Cumberland Conference of SDA
23.	Musa Yo-Salem Ayodo	Medical Missionary Movement International team member	Georgia Cumberland Conference of SDA
24.	Jane Aduke Ndira	Head Deaconess	Better Living Kisumu

Pastor Silfano's sister, Herina Okuom, lived and died a Seventh-day Adventist. Before her demise, she donated land to the church, where Milimani SDA Church, in Migori, is built. His other sister, Keziah Nyangolo, has a rich history of her struggles to establish an Adventist Church in Ajigo, Sakwa, in

The ministry

Bondo District of Siaya County which I wish to highlight to demonstrate the Akumus' commitment to the faith.

Keziah Nyangolo was born in 1908 and named after her late uncle, Nyangolo son of Opapa, who died mysteriously and suddenly when he returned home from military service to mourn his nephew. She was born prematurely and villagers called her *oboge* or *bogno,* referring to her premature birth. Most of her childhood she lived in her uncle's home, in Uyoma Kokwiri, where she learnt to read and write, excelling in Christian Education. She was baptized into the Anglican Church. She married Julius Onyango, of Sakwa Ajigo, in a colorful wedding in Kisumu, presided over by Rev. Reuben Omulo. They had the following children: Otuoma, Edward Otieno, Silpah Okech, Agalo, Eliud Mijema, Eunice Anyango, Jacob Ochieng, Ruth Aluoch and Jaconia Awili. The couple was strict and became devoted Anglican Church members.

In mid-1941, Keziah visited her brother Silfano in Gem during a camp meeting of the Adventists. Pastor Ishmael Opande, who was an inspector of schools, conducted it. It was at this meeting that she heard and accepted the Adventist message. But knowing how harsh her husband was, and his attitude toward the Adventist faith, Silfano warned it would not be smooth sailing for her because the man was an ardent member of the Anglican Church. When she returned to her home in Sakwa, she prepared a place of prayer in the bushes near the home, where she sought the Lord's guidance in the evenings, day time and morning. Her resolve was strong and there was no looking back, because God had touched her with His love!

Before the first Sabbath, after the camp meeting, she was disturbed day and night. She had nightmares, drums pounding in her head and hallucinations. Come Saturday, she was forced

Triumph Through Faith

by her husband to go to the garden to harvest maize. There, she collapsed and was unconscious for some time. This was an indication that God did not want her to work on a Saturday. For the next few weeks she continued to have dreams and visions about the child she was carrying and where she should fellowship. In one such dream she was directed to go to Kamnara SDA Church to worship there. It didn't make sense to her but she obeyed nonetheless.

Her behavior and demeanor, around that time, was that of someone possessed by evil spirits. She could tell people who came to see her where they had been and what they had been doing. As she got more hysterical, her husband and those attending to her decided to relocate her to her mother-in-law's deserted home, but the spirit rejected this outright and the idea was shelved. Her physical health deteriorated. Her husband tried everything, including charms from witchdoctors to turn her round, but nothing came of those efforts. Even a Sheikh from the Coast was brought in, but he did not reverse her declining condition. She continued to be hysterical and to waste away.

One day her husband got fed up with her. He tied her legs with a rope and threw her out of the house. At night, in the cold and tied, weak and frail as she was, she requested that Matthias Okoko and Gamaliel Odundo, the only Adventists around, come and pray for her. Her husband refused. The devil and her husband in equal measure tormented her. Anything Adventist was not acceptable to him. Eventually, though, her husband allowed the two servants of God to come and pray after a doctor examined and found her mentally normal. The two men later prayed for her and a miracle happened. Her feeble hands, which had hitherto been paralyzed, straightened and became normal. After a couple of days, her dreams and hallucinations stopped

The ministry

and she regained her full health. Thereafter, her husband, fearing that she may become mentally ill again, allowed her to worship her God the way she wished to.

Pastor Joel Omer and Pastor Mudaspark baptized Keziah in 1942 at a camp meeting in Maliera. On her return, wind blew off all the thatched structures in the home and this disturbed the husband a lot. As a result, he sought the services of a witchdoctor who advised him to look for a tortoise with a tick to keep in the home. When he brought the tortoise, she took it and threw it away. It was a dramatic act of faith that the husband took note of and would think about for days to come.

Not too long after that display of faith, at an evangelistic crusade of the Anglican Church in Usenge, her husband accepted the Lord and was saved into that faith. He later apologized to her for the way he had treated her. And remarkably, from the day he returned from Usenge he never chased away Adventists who came to his home to worship. He worshipped in the Anglican Church but allowed her to worship as an Adventist. It marked the end of bitter religious wars between Keziah and her husband. Salvation had come. Indeed, the Lord took note of his conversion and allowed the first Adventist Church to be built on his and Naboth Kwaka's land, in Ajigo. But eventual intrigues between the Anglicans, who were the majority, and Adventists, forced the church's relocation to its present site.

Through the efforts of Keziah Nyangolo and Dorcas Akoth, Ajigo people have an Adventist Church today. Julius Onyango, though, lived and died an Anglican. Keziah and her children remained Adventists. Ajigo Adventist Church, which Keziah helped establish, has produced the following Sabbath schools: Akala, Akado, Mabinju and Ndori. Women, who are the majority, manage the church and its offshoots.

SCHEDULE OF KEZIAH NYANGOLO'S DESCENDANT WHO HOLD/HELD POSITIONS IN THE SDA CHURCH

NO	NAME	POSITION	CHURCH
1.	Late Eliud Mijema	Elder	Ajigo SDA Church
2.	Lilly E.A. Ochieng	Deaconess	Milimani SDA, Migori
3.	Prof. Jacob J.J. Ochieng Konyango	Church development Chairperson	Ajigo Church
4.	Ruth A. Kinya	Deaconess	Nairobi Central
5.	Julius Onyango Ochieng	Ordained Minister of the SDA Church	

Based on the work the Lord did through Keziah, it is evident that He did not only work with missionaries, pastors and evangelists, but with whoever He chose. Once Keziah accepted Him, she defied her husband, the villagers and the Anglican Church to become a trailblazer of faith for the Seventh Day Adventists. She was not afraid and is today awaiting the glorious trumpet sound that will awaken all those who slept in Christ.

10

ATTRIBUTES

"...Be strong and courageous. Do not be terrified; do not be discouraged; for the LORD your God will be with you wherever you go." Joshua 1:9 (NIV)

Scientists would like us to believe that half a billion tiny male reproductive cells are deposited inside the female by the male at any time of intercourse and only one which swims fastest finds the female ovum and fertilizes it. The fact is that the single cell that made you had to out-swim half a billion, less one, cells. Any of the half a billion less one, your potential brothers and sisters, could have been born in your place had that one special cell not fertilized that one ovum that produced you. *In essence, half a billion less one humans had to forego life to give way for you to be born.*

Pastor Silfano, like any other human being, came into this world through the same process. That single night. That single act did not produce any other person but Pastor Silfano. Like all of us, he was special and his father's cell had fought, kicked and shoved to reach the mother's ovum to produce him. His presence in this planet, like the presence of all of us, was not only special, but was a miracle. We miraculously find ourselves born male or female. We have neither the choice of when to be born, nor of skin pigmentation, nor of gender.

We are chosen!

Pastor Silfano was chosen and the timing of his birth was precise and unique. It was the right time for someone who had been chosen by God to champion the interests of his people to be born. Consider what God told Jeremiah in Jeremiah 1:5:

"Before I formed you in the womb I knew you, before you were born I set you apart..." (NIV)

God knew Pastor Silfano before He formed him in his mother's womb and set him apart for the purpose of liberating His people.

Paul, in Galatians 1:15, said:

But even before I was born, God chose me and called me by his marvelous grace. (NLT)

The same could be said of Pastor Silfano. Even before he was born God called him and entrusted a task to him. He had set him apart to be the deliverer of his oppressed people. He could not have been born at a better time as the oppression of his people would peak as he turned thirty, an age bracket after teenage, when one is full of vitality and thinks he can move the world. It is the age of invincibility, the age when one can pick up a fight with anybody or face any adversary thinking he is indestructible. This was the frame of mind Pastor Silfano was in when the emancipation began in earnest. He was ready to take on the oppressors!

Like Samson, who was chosen by God and nurtured to protect the Israelites from Philistine attacks, Silfano was chosen, protected and brought up by God to protect Jo-Umani and

Attributes

the entire Ojwando people, who God had chosen to bring the Adventist faith to Central Kavirondo and to spread the gospel to the whole of Western Kenya and beyond. Like Moses, who was chosen to lead the Israelites out of Egyptian bondage, young Silfano was chosen by the Almighty God to lead his people from not only the spiritual bondage of the Anglican Church, but also from the backbreaking oppression of the Ojuodhi people. But just what were his attributes? What was the force that propelled him into the realms of success and heroism? These questions, when answered, will reveal who Pastor Silfano really was.

An abandoned child is like a rudderless ship. He can neither move forward, sideways nor backward. He will stand right there because there is no force to propel him in any direction. Pastor Silfano was lucky to have had a father and a good one at that to shape his character. He borrowed heavily from his unyielding fearless father.

He learned these attributes:

Discipline

Industry

Cheerfulness

Contentment

Service

Commitment

Determination

Fearlessness

His father valued discipline and strove to impart this attribute in his children. Pastor Silfano told me his father was a no nonsense fellow. He expected his children to know the dos and the don'ts even without being taught. Like animals, they were expected to learn by instinct. If they failed to *pick* what they had to do or not do they were whipped, thus being punished for offences they did not know anything about. The tasks to be performed didn't consist of much: herding livestock, tying and untying sheep and goats and cleaning the sheep's, goats' and calves' pen. If a child mastered these and set himself on a routine he was safe. Silfano learned quickly and had few problems with his harsh father. But it was a completely different scenario for his brothers, who refused to adapt fast enough or at all. Theirs was a tale of misery as some of their behavior later brought curses to them and their descendants.

It was this kind of discipline that Pastor Silfano embraced and perfected. It did not only shape his life, but helped shape the lives of his children and those who came under his influence and direct contact. He first disciplined himself, and then was able to discipline others. During those days the whip spoke louder than words. Discipline was a communal responsibility; you were whipped not only by your father but also by any elder who happened to find you doing something wrong. This had the effect of instilling discipline in the children. Pastor Silfano did not spare the whip and thus did not spoil his children. He was not only disciplined, he was also a disciplinarian. There were certain things his children could not do. They could not go to local dances and could not loiter around. They could not return home late. They had no sleepovers or dates. They could only go to church, and to fetch water or firewood.

He learned to be industrious. Hard work is one of the three pillars of a whole and complete life. The other two are book knowledge and spiritual knowledge. Pastor Silfano and hard work were inseparable. He developed a culture of hard work. Wherever he was, he was doing something. He hated indolence. This was one of the virtues he passed on to his children, who

Attributes

prospered because of it. When he was not in the farm, he was herding, cleaning the homestead or at his desk preparing the next day's sermon. He ensured he had his children working with him side by side on these chores.

He reminded himself constantly of an adage stating thus: *An idle mind is the devil's workshop.* Indeed, idle people hatch all heinous crimes. People who are gainfully engaged do not have the time and luxury of planning crimes. He must have been reading the wise words of Solomon virtually every morning, in Proverbs 14:23:

All hard work brings a profit, but mere talk leads only to poverty. (NIV)

As a minister of the gospel, those words must have encouraged and pushed him to make work part of his life. This helped him live a healthier and longer life.

Cheerfulness was his hallmark. He was a happy man during his evangelism years. He had fought the good fight before and won. He had no regrets at all. But what yardstick does one use in measuring happiness, or determining whether one is happy or not? For the sake of the youth, let's answer that question.

For one to be happy at work one must be: Able to commence and do work under one's own initiative and steam; Careful to maintain respect and esteem for other people; Able to stand on his own and take responsibility for his actions, conscious of the fact that happiness comes to those with a purpose-driven life.

Pastor Silfano was all these put together. This demeanor helped him overcome the ups and downs of life and helped him become a good father and a good grandfather. He realized that happiness could be pursued and found. It was something that flowed from a Christian life and the fear of God.

His human limitations notwithstanding, he strove to be perfect and to be a mirror through which others looked to

Triumph Through Faith

measure their perfection. Those who emulated his cheerfulness have had it easy in their endeavors and have succeeded in their undertakings. Those who are cheerful and wear a constant smile never develop wrinkles on their faces. Indeed, Pastor Silfano never had wrinkles on his face; he had peace. He approached whatever he did with soberness and commitment. His concentration was admirable and never deviated from his set goal. Whereas other leaders were jumpy and undecided, Pastor Silfano, once he had his feet on the ground, moved forward steadily. The words of Paul in Philippians 4:11-13 echoed in his mind:

I am not saying this because I am in need, for I have learned to be content whatever the circumstances. I know what it is to be in need, and I know what it is to have plenty. I have learned the secret of being content in any and every situation, whether well fed or hungry, whether living in plenty or in want. I can do everything through him who gives me strength. (NIV)

Once one learns to approach things or issues with a levelheaded mind, one would have learned the secret of contentment. Pastor Silfano, like the apostle Paul, learned it and went about his business in comfort and peace. The secret about contentment was that it aided good health. Listen to these words of wisdom in Proverbs 14:30:

A heart at peace gives life to the body, but envy rots the bones. (NIV)

No wonder Pastor Silfano was blessed with a long life and tons of experience, because he was contented and had a peaceful life.

Selfless service to other people was Pastor Silfano's goal. He worked tirelessly to improve the living conditions of his people and his family. Everybody has a God-given responsibility to help those who are less fortunate attain a level of respectability.

Attributes

Pastor Silfano understood this more than anybody and put it to practice with admirable success. He also put his energy in the service of God. Wherever he evangelized, he left a positive mark and was liked by his flock. He helped establish many Adventist churches. They were: Sota, which later moved to Ahango, Kosele, where he even used his salary to pay teachers, Nyandago, Kolwal, Nyaduong', Pith Nyadundo, Wikodongo, Sagegi, Achuth A (Got Kayayo), Achuth B (Wibware), Achuth C (Ore) and Anding'o. Although his postings took him to more remote areas of lower Nyanza, he was neither discouraged nor disappointed; he knew he was in the ministry to serve God's people. As long as there were people to be served, he would go!

I recall the day I went to one such place to see and consult with him over an issue. He was not at the station and nobody knew where he was. I decided to walk into a neighboring home to inquire his whereabouts. Since it was past midday, the sun was coming down hard and the heat was intense. It looked like it had not rained in a long time. The neighbors had no idea where he had gone. But just as I was talking to my host, my wife walked in. I had left her in the car, but she could not bear the heat and decided to follow me to ask for water. She asked for water and suddenly I also felt thirsty and asked the host to make it two. He dashed into his house and came out with two bottles of Fanta and two glasses and offered these to us. Those who have been in hot places know that sodas don't quench thirst. This was exactly how we felt after taking our Fantas. We still felt thirsty. We thanked him for the sodas, but politely inquired if we could get water to flush the soda down.

"You must have travelled from far?" he said in a manner suggesting if we were locals we would not have asked for water.

"Yes, we have," I said.

He nodded then said, "Water is a rare and expensive commodity around here. It is easier and cheaper to get a bottle of soda than a glass of water."

Such were the hardship areas Pastor Silfano served without ever complaining. The church leadership in Gendia, and later in Ranen, liked him for that selfless service to God's people. It was his calling!

His commitment to his work and undertakings was unparalleled. Once he set his eyes on something there was neither deviation nor diversion. When you are starting out to do something, psyche yourself for success and never leave room for failure. The day you start out is not the time to prepare. Assemble your entire arsenal for battle, and then move swiftly for quick victory. Pastor Silfano had this in mind all the time. Like Christ's disciples, who committed themselves to Jesus by leaving their occupations to follow Him, he committed himself to his work and to his God—and never looked back.

He followed the example of Paul in 2 Timothy 2:10:

Therefore I endure everything for the sake of the elect that they too may obtain the salvation that is in Christ Jesus, with eternal glory. (NIV)

Pastor Silfano committed himself to a worthy cause and stayed the course to the end. His commitment, however, could not match the supreme commitment of Christ as our redeemer, who paid the ultimate price and suffered the ultimate penalty for our sins. In John 3:16, the ringing cry of the ages is proclaimed with clarity.

For God so loved the world that He gave His only begotten son, that whoever believes in Him should not perish but have everlasting life. (NKJV)

It was by the grace of God that He sent His son to come and save the world. The son committed Himself to this course and

Attributes

paid with His life. Christ's sacrifice was for all of us. No other sacrifice will be required for the salvation of mankind. Writing to the Hebrews, Paul had this to say in Hebrews 10:5-7 and 10:

V5 Therefore, when He came into the world, He said: "Sacrifice and offering you did not desire, but a body you have prepared for me. V6 In burnt offerings and sacrifices for sin you have no pleasure. V7 Then I said, 'Behold, I have come—In the volume of the book it is written of Me—to do Your will, O God.'" V10 By that will we have been sanctified through the offering of the body of Jesus Christ once for all. (NKJV)

Pastor Silfano's commitment and sacrifice was a pale shadow of and incomparable to the commitment and sacrifice Jesus made to save mankind. It is man's responsibility to seek the LORD as Isaiah points out in Isaiah 55:6-7:

Seek the LORD while he may be found; call on him while he is near. Let the wicked forsake his way and the evil man his thoughts. Let him turn to the Lord and He will have mercy on him, and to our God, for he will freely pardon. (NIV)

If mankind earnestly seeks the Lord with all his heart, the gracious Lord will pardon his sins. The Apostle Paul emphasizes this in Romans 10:12-13, where he says:

For there is no difference between Jew and Gentile—the same Lord is Lord of all and richly blesses all who call on Him, for, "Everyone who calls on the name of the Lord will be saved." (NIV)

So everyone, the saved, the church members and the unbelievers, are exhorted to listen and understand what Paul tells the Romans: Everyone who calls on the name of the lord will be saved. Whether black, white or yellow, if one truly wants salvation Paul reveals the secret.

Pastor Silfano's determination and firmness was the envy of many. His work ethics and the way he went around doing his tasks left no doubt that he was resolute in whatever he did. He dreamt big and worked towards those dreams with charisma and zeal. He wasn't complacent and never procrastinated. His heart never turned back nor his feet strayed from the Lord's path. He was in the Lord and the Lord in him since he had discarded the gods his ancestors worshipped and now worshipped Him faithfully. His heart was steadfast in worship and he had his eyes fixed on the cross.

His faith could not be shaken. Like a tree by the riverside whose roots reach the water and help it grow strong, steadfast and firm, he was strong and unshaken. At the back of his mind was the warning in Proverbs 24:10:

If you faint in the day of adversity, your strength is small.

Like Job, he braced himself for troubles and turbulences.

Brace yourself like a man; I will question you, and you shall answer me. Job 38:3 (NKJV)

Pastor Silfano was fearless, but within the human parameters. He could approach and talk to anybody even if the topic was acrimonious. Like the courage of Joshua and Caleb, who convinced the Israelites that the land God had promised them was good despite what their co-explorers said, Pastor Silfano was ready to die for the truth. He was daring like Gideon, with his three hundred elite army, who God used in defeating the Midianites. And he had the boldness of Nehemiah, who when he was told people would come at night to kill him and should go and hide in the temple refused to do so.

The fearlessness of Pastor Silfano was a reflection of the bravery of Esther, a Jewish girl who became queen to King Xerxes. A plot to annihilate the Jews was discovered and reported to her to do something about. Although she was prohibited from seeing the king at that time, after fasting and praying she decided to approach the king. After observing the

Attributes

palace protocol, she made a petition to the king, which the king accepted, and saved the Jews from Haman's evil and heinous designs.

Let me wind this down. Pastor Silfano's boldness, frankness and courage made him a legend among his people. Paul, writing to Titus in Titus 2:15, captures this boldness and courage vividly:

These, then, are the things you should teach, encourage and rebuke with all authority. Do not let anyone despise you. (NKJV)

That was the type of bold leadership God bestowed on Pastor Silfano. Facing the might of the Anglican Church those days was no picnic. Only Pastor Silfano faced them and lived to tell the story. Facing the colonial administration was equally an uphill task, but Pastor Silfano faced them and freed his people from subjugation.

Other than traits acquired from his father, Silfano had personal characteristics. Some were inborn, others acquired. He had the unique character of humility. He could not provoke or antagonize anybody. Unlike his father, he was not loud. When annoyed, he simply kept quiet and walked away. He respected people and their views, and never meddled in other people's affairs.

To some, he was tough and stubborn or even exacting, but these were within the parameters of a good leader. He shied away from arrogance and steered clear from being domineering. He preferred to identify with the lowly than dine with the high and the mighty. People would notice his presence only when he spoke or prayed for them. He had a high pitched tone that was distinct and unmistakable. He was gracious and treated all people as sons and daughters of God. He was aware of what God said in Matthew 5:5:

Triumph Through Faith

Blessed are the meek, for they shall inherit the earth. (NKJV)

A lot has been said about giving and the benefits thereof. Pastor Silfano was not only merciful, but a noble giver. He was considerate and minded the plight of other people. He was his brother's keeper. His magnanimity was immeasurable and was demonstrated by instances of real-life experiences. When God gave him Adventism, he worked hard to persuade his brothers, sisters, neighbors and countrymen to share in the amazing joys. Some did, some didn't. The disparity in prosperity for those who did, compared to those who didn't, is there for all to see.

When God gave him the first opportunity among equals to get an education, he did not just sit back and enjoy his newfound status. He would have continued working at the Tribunal, but he was sympathetic to the plight of his people and resigned his Tribunal position to fight for their freedom.

When, like Joshua and Caleb, God gave him the opportunity to go to the Promised Land and returned convinced that the land was good for settlement, he did not just settle after acquiring land, he went out of his way to invite his relatives, friends, kinsmen and neighbors to cross over and join him. In fact, he wanted as many of his people to come as were able to. Those who agreed and migrated lived like nobles in the new land. He was not generous to get cheap publicity or for self-aggrandizement, he did it from the bottom of his heart.

Have you ever experienced the feeling of satisfaction after you went out and saved one from a burning house or one trapped inside a car in an accident? Or have you given food to a starving stranger who passed by your home? If you haven't, try it. Put yourself in the position of the person who needs help and see if you would need help if you were in that position. Then whatever you give or volunteer to do, don't expect payback. That was Pastor Silfano. In being generous consistently, he

Attributes

must have been aware of the encouraging words of the Psalmist, in Psalms 37:26:

They are always generous and lend freely; their children will be blessed. (NIV)

Because of his magnanimity, his children, grandchildren and great grandchildren are blessed indeed. Among them are teachers, professors, lawyers, evangelists, parastatal heads, government officials, NGO heads, and businessmen and women. The Lord indeed is faithful!

In giving freely and willingly to the poor and the needy, Pastor Silfano must have been aware that giving to the poor is lending to the LORD. This is captured in Proverbs 19:17 which says:

He who is kind to the poor lends to the LORD, and He will reward him for what he has done. (NIV)

And Solomon's wise words in Proverbs 3:27-28:

Do not withhold good from those to whom it is due, when it is in the power of your hand to do so. Do not say to your neighbor, "Go, and come back and tomorrow I will give it," when you have it with you. (NKJV).

By the authority of Psalms 37:26, we have seen that those who are generous their children will be blessed like Pastor Silfano's. But how about the giver? Does he also stand to benefit? Proverbs 22:9, has the answer:

A generous man will himself be blessed, for he shares his food with the poor. (NIV)

Pastor Silfano lived this and was abundantly blessed. And Paul, writing to the Corinthians, shows that generosity will be rewarded: 2 Corinthians 9:6-11, says this:

But this I say: He who sows sparingly will also reap sparingly, and he who sows bountifully will also reap bountifully. So let each one give

Triumph Through Faith

as purposes in his heart, not grudgingly or of necessity; for God loves a cheerful giver. And God is able to make all grace abound toward you, that you, always having all sufficiency in all things, may have abundance for every good work. As it is written: "He has dispersed abroad, He has given to the poor; His righteousness endures forever." Now may He who supplies seed to the sower, and bread for food, supply and multiply the seed you have sown and increase the fruits of your righteousness, while you are enriched in everything for all liberality, which causes thanksgiving through us to God. (NKJV)

Pastor Silfano's benevolence guarantees him the following bounty harvests:

Blessings to his offspring, including the offspring of his offspring

Blessings to himself here on earth

Blessings to himself in heaven

Blessings to his property of all kind

I have dwelt on the pastor's attributes because many of us fail to see the relevance of benevolence today. I want us to see this as a key attribute in leadership and Christianity. But maybe it would be better if Christ talks about this Himself. Let Him speak...

A rich young man approached Jesus and asked him what he could do to get eternal life. Jesus told him, *"Obey the commandments"*

"All these I have kept," the young man said. *"What do I still lack?"* Matthew 19:20 (NIV)

"If you want to be perfect, go, sell your possessions and give to the poor, and you will have treasure in heaven. Then come, follow me." Matthew 19:21 (NIV).

The rich young man went away crestfallen as he could not imagine parting ways with his possessions. The disciples

Attributes

who were present and were following that conversation were astonished. Jesus had raised the bar so high. They asked, *"Who then can be saved?"*

Jesus looked at them and said, *"With man this is impossible, but with God all things are possible."*

This was deep. Jesus made a critical point here. He wanted man to know that the path to salvation ran through Him and not the earthly efforts of feeble man. Pastor Silfano was keenly aware of this. His perfection was anchored only in human definition, where he became a living example and a model to people who wanted to join the heaven-bound train. He was not perfect like the angels. He was not perfect as the saints we read about in the Bible. He was not perfect like the heroes and heroines of the Old Testament. But he was full of the spirit and knew that the human definition of perfection was only relevant in so far as it was attached to God's.

Pastor Silfano's spiritual character was self-evident; he served the Lord with commitment and dedication for many years and died in the Lord. He believed that God did not put him here on earth to be ordinary. He became a spiritually inspired leader and demonstrated he was a leader of leaders. The purity of the heart and the beauty of the character are a measure of greatness of a leader. Pastor Silfano's heart and character confirmed him as an effective leader, a devout Christian and a role model. He yearned for the Lord in prayer and the Lord heard him. He endeavored to be holy and righteous to God and God lifted him. His righteousness was conspicuous and anybody could see it. He praised God for protecting him against his adversaries. He praised God for lifting him up and placing him on higher ground. He praised God for giving him the knowledge and wisdom that informed his every step for the struggle of his people and the struggle to be afloat. He praised God for the earthly bounty that enabled him to be benevolent. He praised and thanked God for the gift of offsprings and prayed that all his descendants would join him in the spaceship to heaven. He praised God for the gift of life itself, for making him believe in himself and making him realize that in the midst of life we are all dead. His was a life of praise!

Paul, writing to the Church in Corinth, said, in 1 Corinthians 1:4-9:

I always thank God for you because of His grace given you in Christ Jesus. For in Him you have been enriched in every way—in all your speaking and in all your knowledge—because our testimony about Christ was confirmed in you. Therefore you do not lack any spiritual gift as you eagerly wait for our Lord Jesus Christ to be revealed. He will keep you strong to the end, so that you will be blameless on the day of our Lord Jesus Christ. God, who has called you into fellowship with His son Jesus Christ our Lord, is faithful. (NIV)

That was the true righteousness in Christ that Pastor Silfano had.

He was always thankful to God for everything, keeping up to date with his tithes and offerings and maintaining a charity coffer from where he pooled funds for the poor. And because Christ our Lord is faithful, He promises to enrich us in every way. We need to realize that the kingdom of God is within us and all we need to do is keep our souls in good health. Like John said in 3 John 1:2:

Dear friend, I pray that you may enjoy good health and that all may go well with you, even as your soul is getting along well. (NIV)

Such was the life of this great leader. He wanted Adventist churches planted in every corner of Central Kavirondo and beyond. He hungered for the Word of God and, when he got it, took it as his marching orders. Because of what he did, his

Attributes

people are today prepared for the hunger prophesied to the Israelites, in particular, and to Christians, in general. Allow me to conclude with that chilling prophetic warning:

Behold days are coming, says the Lord God, that I will send a famine on the land, not a famine of bread, nor a thirst for water, but for hearing. (Amos 8:11, NKJV)

I will say no more!

11

ARRIVAL OF SEVENTH-DAY ADVENTISM IN KENYA

Therefore go and make disciples of all nations, baptizing them in the name of the Father and of the Son and of the Holy Spirit, and teaching them to obey everything I have commanded you. And surely I am with you always, to the very end of the age. Matthew 28:19-20 (NIV)

Previously I highlighted how Pastor Silfano, leading a team of great elders, brought the Seventh-day Adventist Church to Central Kavirondo, in 1939. I narrated the struggles they went through and the joy and optimism that followed their success. I reiterated that Adventism was unique because it was the only one of its kind, at the time, worshipping on Saturday in Central Kavirondo. I mentioned in passing the origin of Sabbath-keeping, but did not connect it to the Seventh-day Adventist denomination. This chapter is intended to make that connection and show, in brief, what Adventism means, what beliefs it upholds, and its organizational structure.

By the authority of the Bible, it is known that the sacredness and sanctity of Sabbath keeping originated at creation, in the Garden of Eden, and that God rested on the seventh day; after completing creation work in six days. He blessed the seventh day and made it holy (Genesis 2:1-3). The Israelites observed the Sabbath before God gave the Ten Commandments to Moses. The story of the Israelites picking manna all week except on the Sabbath is a testimony to that fact (Exodus 16:13-27). It's also known that prophets ratified observance of the Sabbath. The Bible is replete with instances of Sabbath keeping or Sabbath breaking. Here are a few examples:

» A Sabbath breaker was to be put to death. (Numbers 15:32-36)

» Jeremiah warned Israelites not to carry a load through the gates of Jerusalem on Sabbath day. (Jeremiah 17:21-27)

» Isaiah warned about Sabbath keeping. (Isaiah 58:13 and 66:22-23)

This is proof that prophets were serious on Sabbath keeping. Indeed, even Jesus observed the Sabbath both at creation and when He came down to save mankind. Luke brings this out in Luke 4:16:

He went to Nazareth, where he had been brought up, and on the Sabbath day he went in to the synagogue as was his custom. And he stood up to read. (NIV)

The Sabbath day commemorates the creation and scriptures exhort us to remember and keep it holy in Exodus 20:8-11 and Deuteronomy 5:12-15. In fact, the Sabbath day is the SEAL of God Almighty. Ezekiel brings this out with clarity.

"...I am the LORD your God; follow my decrees and be careful to keep my laws. Keep my Sabbaths holy, that they may be a sign between us. Then you will know that I am the LORD your God." Ezekiel 20:19-20 (NIV)

But Ezekiel is not alone; Nehemiah is just as forceful in his warning about the place of the Sabbath in God's heart and how we should relate to it. My word is: heed Nehemiah's warning to the Israelites about desecrating the Sabbath given in Nehemiah 13:15-19.

After the resurrection and ascension of Jesus, the disciples continued to observe the Sabbath. Paul preached to the Jews and Gentiles on the Sabbath in Antioch (Acts 13:14-15, 42-43). Paul, Timothy and Silas preached to the women in Philippi, among them Lydia, on Sabbath day (Acts 16:12-15). The Sabbath, therefore, is rest for the people of God (Hebrews 4:1-11), a seal by which God's people are identified. That being the case, what distinguishes the Seventh-day Adventist Church from the rest of Christian churches?

Let's get right down to it.

The difference is in the beliefs. The Adventists accept the Bible as the only creed and hold certain fundamental beliefs to be the teachings of the Holy Scriptures. The beliefs are not cast in stone; they are revisable as the Holy Spirit leads the church to a fuller understanding of Bible truth. I want to list them verbatim for the benefit of those who have never read them in the book known as *Fundamental Beliefs*.

1. **Holy Scriptures:**

    The Holy Scriptures, the Old and the New Testaments, are the written Word of God, given by divine inspiration through holy men of God who spoke and wrote as the Holy Spirit moved them. In this Word, God has committed to man the knowledge necessary for salvation. The Holy Scriptures is the infallible revelation of His will. They are the standard of character, the test of experience, the authoritative revealer of doctrines, and the trustworthy record of God's acts in history. (2 Peter 1:20, 21; 2 Timothy 3:16, 17; Psalms 119:105; Proverbs 30:5, 6; Isaiah 8:20; John 17:17; 1 Thessalonians 2:13; Hebrews 4:12.)

2. Trinity:

There is one God: Father, Son and Holy Spirit, a unity of three coeternal Persons. God is immortal, all-powerful, all knowing, above all, and ever present. He is infinite and beyond human comprehension, yet known through His self-revelation. He is forever worthy of worship, adoration, and service by the whole creation.

(Deuteronomy 6:4; Matthew 28:19; 2 Corinthians 13:14; Ephesians 4:4-6; 1 Peter 1:2; 1 Timothy 1:17; Revelation 14:7.)

3. Father:

God the eternal Father is the Creator, Source, Sustainer, and Sovereign of all creation. He is just and holy, merciful and gracious, slow to anger, and abounding in steadfast love and faithfulness. The qualities and powers exhibited in the Son and the Holy Spirit are also revelations of the Father. (Genesis 1:1; Revelation 4:11; 1 Corinthians 15:28; John 3:16; 1 John 4:8; 1 Timothy 1:17; Exodus 34:6, 7; John 14:9.)

4. Son:

God the eternal Son became incarnate in Jesus Christ. Through him all things were created, the character of God is revealed, the salvation of humanity is accomplished, and the world is judged. Forever truly God, He became also truly man, Jesus the Christ. He was conceived of the Holy Spirit and born of the Virgin Mary. He lived and experienced temptation as a human being, but perfectly exemplified the righteousness and love of God. By His miracles He manifested God's power and was attested as God's promised Messiah.

He suffered and died voluntarily on the cross for our sins and in our place, was raised from the dead, and ascended to minister in the heavenly sanctuary on our behalf. He will come again in glory for the final deliverance of His people and the restoration of all things. (John 1:1-3, 14; Colossians 1:15-19; John 10:30; 14:9; Romans 6:23; 2 Corinthians 5:17-19; John 5:22; Luke 1:35; Philippians 2:5-11; Hebrews 2:9-18; 1 Corinthians 15:3, 4; Hebrews 8:1, 2; John 14:1-3.)

5. Holy Spirit:

God the eternal Spirit was active with the Father and the Son in creation, incarnation, and redemption. He inspired the writers of Scripture. He filled Christ's life with power. He draws and convicts human beings; and those who respond He renews and transforms into the image of God. Sent by the Father and the Son to be always with His children, He extends spiritual gifts to the church, empowers it to bear witness to Christ, and in harmony with the Scriptures leads it into all truth. (Genesis 1:1, 2; Luke 1:35; 4:18; Acts 10:38; 2 Peter 1:21; 2 Corinthians 3:18; Ephesians 4:11, 12; Acts 1:8; John 14:16-18, 26; 15:26, 27; 16:7-13.)

6. Creation:

God is Creator of all things, and has revealed in Scripture the authentic account of His creative activity. In six days the Lord made "the heaven and the earth" and all living things upon the earth, and rested on the seventh day of that first week. Thus He established the Sabbath as a perpetual memorial of his completed creative work. The first man and woman were made in the image of God as the crowning work of Creation, given dominion over the world, and charged with responsibility to care for it. When the world was finished it was "very good," declaring the glory of God. (Genesis 1:2; Exodus 20:8-11; Psalms 19:1-6; 33:6, 9; 104; Hebrews 11:3.)

7. **Nature of Man:**
   Man and woman were made in the image of God with individuality, the power and freedom to think and to do. Though created free beings, each is an indivisible unity of body, mind and spirit, dependent upon God for life and breath and all else. When our first parents disobeyed God, they denied their dependence upon Him and fell from their high position under God. The image of God in them was marred and they became Subject to death. Their descendants share this fallen nature and its consequences. They are born with weaknesses and tendencies to evil. But God in Christ reconciled the world to Himself and by His Spirit restores in penitent mortals the image of their Maker. Created for the glory of God, they are called to love Him and one another, and to care for their environment. (Genesis 1:26-28; 2:7; Psalms 8:4-8; Acts 17:24-28; Genesis 3; Psalms 51:5; Romans 5:12-17; 2 Corinthians 5:19, 20; Psalms 51:10; 1 John 4:7, 8, 11, 20; Genesis 2:15.)

8. **Great Controversy:**
   All humanity is now involved in a great controversy between Christ and Satan regarding the character of God, His law, and His sovereignty over the universe. This conflict originated in heaven when a created being, endowed with freedom of choice, in self-exaltation became Satan, God's adversary, and led into rebellion a portion of the angels. He introduced the spirit of rebellion into this world when he

led Adam and Eve into sin. This human sin resulted in the distortion of the image of God in humanity, the disordering of the created world, and its eventual devastation at the time of the worldwide flood. Observed by the whole creation, this world became the arena of the universal conflict, out of which the God of love will ultimately be vindicated. To assist His people in this controversy, Christ sends the Holy Spirit and the loyal angels to guide, protect, and sustain them in the way of salvation. (Revelation 12:4-9; Isaiah 14:12-14; Ezekiel 28:12-18; Genesis 3: Romans 1:19-32; 5:12-21; 8:19-22; Genesis 6-8; 2 Peter 3:6; 1 Corinthians 4:9; Hebrews 1:14.)

9. **Life, Death, and Resurrection of Christ:**
In Christ's life of perfect obedience to God's will, His suffering, death, and resurrection, God provided the only means of atonement for human sin, so that those who by faith accept this atonement may have eternal life, and the whole creation may better understand an infinite and holy love of the Creator. This perfect atonement vindicates the righteousness of God's law and the graciousness of His character; for it both condemns our sin and provides for our forgiveness. The death of Christ is substitutionary and expiatory, reconciling and transforming. The resurrection of Christ proclaims God's triumph over the forces of evil, and for those who accept the atonement assures their final victory over sin and death. It declares the Lordship of Jesus Christ, before whom every knee in heaven and on earth will bow. (John 3:16; Isaiah 53; 1 Peter 2:21, 22; 1 Corinthians 15:3, 4, 20-22; 2 Corinthians 5:14, 15, 19-21; Romans 1:4; 3:25; 4:25; 8:3, 4; 1 John 2:2; 4:10; Colossians 2:15; Philippians 2:6-11.)

10. Experience of Salvation:

In infinite love and mercy God made Christ, who knew no sin, to be sin for us, so that in Him we might be made the righteousness of God. Led by the Holy Spirit we sense our need, acknowledge our sinfulness, repent of our transgressions, and exercise faith in Jesus as Lord and Christ, as Substitute and Example. This faith, which receives salvation, comes through the divine power of the Word and is the gift of God's grace. Through Christ we are justified, adopted as God's sons and daughters, and delivered from the lordship of sin. Through the Spirit we are born again and sanctified; the Spirit renews our minds, writes God's law of love in our hearts, and we are given the power to live a holy life. Abiding in him, we become partakers of the divine nature and have the assurance of salvation now and in the judgment. (2 Corinthians 5:17-21; John 3:16; Galatians 1:4; 4:4-7; Titus 3:3-7; John 16:8; Galatians 3:13, 14; 1 Peter 2:21, 22; Romans 10:17; Luke 17:5; Mark 9:23, 24; Ephesians 2:5-10; Romans 3:21-26; Colossians 1:13, 14; Romans 8:14-17; Galatians 3:26; John 3:3-8; 1 Peter 1:23; Romans 12:2; Hebrews 8:7-12; Ezekiel 36:25-27; 2 Peter 1:3, 4; Romans 8:1-4; 5:6-10.)

11. Growing in Christ:

By his death on the cross, Jesus triumphed over the forces of evil. He who subjugated the demonic spirits during His earthly ministry has broken their power and made certain their ultimate doom. Jesus' victory gives us victory over the evil forces that still seek to control us, as we walk with Him in peace, joy and assurance of His love. Now the Holy Spirit dwells within us and empowers us. Continually committed to Jesus as our Savior and Lord, we are set free from the burden of our past deeds.

No longer do we live in the darkness, fear of evil powers, ignorance, and meaninglessness of our former way of life. In this new freedom in Jesus, we are called to grow into the likeness of His character, communing with Him daily in prayer, feeding on His Word, meditating on it and on His providence, singing His praises, gathering together for worship, and participating in the mission of the church. As we give ourselves in loving service to those around us and in witnessing to His salvation, His constant presence with us through the Spirit transforms every moment and every task into a Spiritual experience. (Psalms 1:1, 2; 23:4; 77:11, 12; Colossians 1:13, 14; 2:6, 14, 15; Luke 10:17-20; Ephesians 5:19, 20; 6:12-18; 1 Thessalonians. 5:23; 2 Peter 2:9; 3:18; 2 Corinthians 3:17, 18; Philippians 3:7-14; 1 Thessalonians 5:16-18; Matthew 20:25-28; John 20:21; Galatians 5:22-25; Romans 8:38, 39; 1 John 4:4; Hebrews 10:25.)

12. Church:

The Church is the community of believers who confess Jesus Christ as Lord and Savior. In continuity with the people of God in Old Testament times, we are called out from the world; and we join together for worship, for fellowship, for instruction in the Word, for the celebration of the Lord's Supper, for service to all mankind, and for the worldwide proclamation of the gospel. The church derives its authority from Christ, who is the incarnate Word, and from the Scriptures, which are the written Word. The church is God's family; adopted by Him as children, its members live on the basis of the new covenant. The church is the body of Christ, a community of faith of which Christ Himself is the Head. The church is the bride for whom

Arrival of Seventh-day Adventism in Kenya

Christ died that He might sanctify and cleanse her. At His return in triumph, He will present her to Himself a glorious church, the faithful of all the ages, the purchase of His blood, not having spot or wrinkle, but holy and without blemish. (Genesis 12:3; Acts 7:38; Ephesians 4:11-15; 3:8-11; Matthew 28:19, 20; 16:13-20; 18:18; Ephesians 2:19-22; 1:22, 23; 5:23-27; Colossians 1:17,18.)

13. Remnant and Its Mission:

The universal church is composed of all who truly believe in Christ, but in the last days, a time of widespread apostasy, a remnant has been called out to keep the commandments of God and the faith of Jesus. This remnant announces the arrival of the judgment hour, proclaims salvation through Christ, and heralds the approach of His second advent. The three angels of Revelation 14 symbolize this proclamation: it coincides with work of judgment in heaven and results in a work of repentance and reform on earth. Every believer is called to have a personal part in this worldwide witness. (Revelations 12:17; 14:6-12; 18:1-4; 2 Corinthians 5:10; Jude 3, 14; 1 Peter 1:16-19; 2 Peter 3:10-14; Revelations 21:1-14.)

14. Unity in the Body of Christ:

The church is one body with many members, called from every nation, kindred, tongue, and people. In Christ we are a new creation; distinctions of race, culture, learning and nationality, and differences between high and low, rich and poor, male and female, must not be divisive among us. We are all equal in Christ, who by one Spirit has bonded us into one fellowship with Him and with one another; we are to serve and be served without partiality or reservation.

Triumph Through Faith

Through the revelation of Jesus Christ in Scriptures we share the same faith and hope, and reach out in one witness to all. This unity has its source in the oneness of the triune God, who has adopted us as His children. (Romans 12:4, 5; 1 Corinthians 12:12-14; Matthew 28:19, 20; Psalms 133:1; 2 Corinthians 5:16, 17; Acts 17:26, 27; Galatians 3:27, 29; Colossians 3:10-15; Ephesians 4:14-16; 4:1-6; John 17:20-23.)

15. Baptism:

By baptism we confess our faith in the death and resurrection of Jesus Christ, and testify of our death to sin and of our purpose to walk in newness of life. Thus we acknowledge Christ as Lord and Savior, become His people, and are received as members by His church. Baptism is a symbol of our union with Christ, the forgiveness of our sins, and our reception of the Holy Spirit. It is by immersion in water and is contingent on an affirmation of faith in Jesus and evidence of repentance of sin. It follows instruction in the Holy Scriptures and acceptance of their teachings (Romans 6:1-6; Colossians 2:12, 13; Acts 16:30-33; 22:16; 2:38; Matthew 28:19, 20.)

16. Lord's Supper:

The Lord's Supper is a participation in the emblems of the body and blood of Jesus as an expression of faith in Him, our Lord and Savior. In this experience of communion Christ is present to meet and strengthen His people. As we partake, we joyfully proclaim the Lord's death until he comes again. Preparation for the Supper includes self-examination, repentance, and confession. The Master ordained the service of foot washing to signify renewed cleansing, to express a willingness to serve one another in Christ-like humility, and to unite our hearts in love. The communion service is open to all believing Christians. (1 Corinthians 10:16, 17; 11:23-30; Matthew 26:17-30; Revelation 3:20; John 6:48-63; 13:1-17.)

17. Spiritual Gifts and Ministries:

God bestows upon all members of His church in every age spiritual gifts, which each member is to employ in loving ministry for the common good of the church and of humanity. Given by the agency of the Holy Spirit, who apportions to each member as He wills, the gifts provide all abilities and ministries needed by the church to fulfill its divinely ordained functions. According to the Scriptures, these gifts include such ministries as faith, healing, prophecy, proclamation, teaching, administration, reconciliation, compassion, and self-sacrificing service and charity for the help and encouragement of people. Some members are called of God and endowed by the Spirit for functions recognized by the church in pastoral, evangelistic, apostolic, and teaching ministries particularly needed to equip the members for service, to build up the church to spiritual maturity, and to foster unity of the faith and knowledge of God. When members employ these spiritual gifts as faithful stewards of God's varied grace, the church is protected from the destructive influence of false doctrine, grows with a growth that is from God, and is built up in faith and love. (Romans 12:4-8; 1 Corinthians 12:9-11, 27, 28; Ephesians 4:8, 11-16; Acts 6:1-7, 1 Timothy 3:1-13; 1 Peter 4: 10, 11.)

18. Gift of Prophecy:

One of the gifts of the Holy Spirit is prophecy. This gift is an identifying mark of the remnant church and was manifested in the ministry of Ellen G. White. As the Lord's messenger, her writings are a continuing and authoritative source of truth, which provide for the church comfort, guidance, instruction and correction. They also make clear that the Bible is the standard by which all teaching and experience must be tested. (Joel 2:28, 29: Acts 2:14-21; Hebrews 1:1-3; Revelation 12:17; 19:10.)

19. Law of God:

The great principles of God's law are embodied in the Ten Commandments and exemplified in the life of Christ. They express God's love, will, and purposes concerning human conduct and relationships and are binding upon all people in every age. These precepts are the basis of God's covenant with His people and the standard in God's judgment. Through the agency of the Holy Spirit they point out sin and awaken a sense of need for a Savior. Salvation is all of grace and not of works, but its fruitage is obedience to the Commandments. This obedience develops Christian character and results in a sense of well-being; it is an evidence of our love for the Lord and our concern for our fellow men. The obedience of faith demonstrates the power of Christ to transform lives, and therefore strengthens Christian witness. (Exodus 20:1-17; Psalms 40:7, 8: Matthew 22:36-40; Deuteronomy 28:1-14; Matthew 5:17-20; Hebrews 8:8-10; John 15:7-10; Ephesians 2:8-10; 1 John 5:3; Romans 8:3, 4; Psalms 19:7-14.)

20. Sabbath:

The beneficent Creator, after the six days of Creation, rested on the seventh day and instituted the Sabbath for all people as a memorial of Creation. The fourth commandment of God's unchangeable law requires the observance of this seventh-day Sabbath as the day of rest, worship, and ministry in harmony with the teaching and practice of Jesus, the Lord of the Sabbath. The Sabbath is a day of delightful communion with God and one another. It is a symbol of our redemption in Christ, a sign of our sanctification, a token of our allegiance, and a foretaste of our eternal future in God's kingdom. The Sabbath is God's perpetual sign of his eternal covenant between Him and His people. Joyful observance of this holy time from evening to evening, sunset to sunset, is a celebration of God's creative and redemptive acts. (Genesis 2:1-3; Exodus 20:8-11; Luke 4:16; Isaiah 56:5, 6; 58:13, 14; Matthew 12:1-12; Exodus 31:13-17; Ezekiel 20:12, 20; Deuteronomy 5:12-15; Hebrews 4:1-11; Leviticus 23:32; Mark 1:32.)

21. Stewardship:

We are God's stewards, entrusted by Him with time and opportunities, abilities and possessions, and the blessings of the earth and its resources. We are responsible to Him for their proper use. We acknowledge God's ownership by faithful service to Him and our fellow men, and by returning tithes and giving offerings for the proclamation of His gospel and the support and growth of His church. Stewardship is a privilege given to us by God for nurture in love and the victory over selfishness and covetousness. The steward rejoices in the blessings that come to others as a result of his faithfulness. (Genesis 1: 26-28; 2:15; 1 Chronicles 29:14; Haggai 1:3-11; Malachi 3:8-12; 1 Corinthians 9:9-14; Matthew 23:23; 2 Corinthians 8:1-15; Romans 15:26, 27.)

22. Christian Behavior:

We are called to be a godly people who think, feel, and act in harmony with the principles of heaven. For the Spirit to recreate in us the character of our Lord we involve ourselves only in those things, which will produce Christ-like purity, health, and joy in our lives. This means that our amusement and entertainment should meet the highest standards of Christian taste and beauty.

While recognizing cultural differences, our dress is to be simple, modest, and neat, befitting those whose true beauty does not consist of outward adornment but in the imperishable ornament of a gentle and quiet spirit.

It also means that because our bodies are the temples of the Holy Spirit, we are to care for them intelligently. Along with adequate exercise and rest, we are to adopt the most healthful diet possible and abstain from the unclean foods identified in the scriptures. Since alcoholic beverages, tobacco, and the irresponsible use of drugs and narcotics are harmful to our bodies, we are to abstain from them as well. Instead, we are to engage in whatever brings our thoughts and bodies into the discipline of Christ, who desires our wholesomeness, joy and goodness. (Romans 12:1, 2; 1 John 2:6; Ephesians 5:1-21; Philippians 4:8; 2 Corinthians 10:5; 6:14-7:1; 1 Peter 3:1-4; 1 Corinthians 6:19, 20; 10:31; Leviticus 11:1-47; 3 John 2.)

23. Marriage and Family:

Marriage was divinely established in Eden and affirmed by Jesus to be a lifelong union between a man and a woman in loving companionship. For the Christian a marriage commitment is to God as well as to the spouse, and should be entered into only between partners who share a common faith. Mutual love, honor, respect, and responsibility are the fabric of this relationship, which is to reflect the love, sanctity, closeness and permanence of the relationship between Christ and His church. Regarding divorce, Jesus taught that the person who divorces a spouse except for fornication, and marries another, commits adultery.

Although some family relationships may fall short of the ideal, marriage partners who fully commit themselves to each other in Christ may achieve loving unity through the guidance of the Spirit and the nurture of the church. God blesses the family and intends that its members shall assist each other toward complete maturity.

Parents are to bring up their children to love and obey the Lord. "By their example and their words they are to teach them that Christ is a loving disciplinarian, ever tender and caring, who wants them to become members of His body, the family of God. Increasing family closeness is one of the earmarks of the final gospel message. (Genesis 2:18-25; Matthew 19:3-9; John 2:1-11; 2 Corinthians 6:14; Ephesians 5:21-33; Matthew 5:31, 32; Mark 10:11, 12; Luke 16:18; 1 Corinthians 7:10, 11; Exodus 20:12; Ephesians 6:1-4; Deuteronomy 6:5-9; Proverbs 22:6; Malachi 4:5, 6.)

24. Christ's Ministry in the Heavenly Sanctuary:

There is a sanctuary in heaven, the true tabernacle, which the Lord set up, and not man. In it, Christ ministers on our behalf, making available to believers the benefits of His atoning sacrifice offered once for all on the cross. He was inaugurated as our great High Priest and began His intercessory ministry at the time of His ascension. In 1844, at the end of the prophetic period of 2300 days, He entered the second and last phase of atoning ministry.

It is a work of investigative judgment that is part of the ultimate disposition of all sin, typified by the cleansing of the ancient Hebrew sanctuary on the Day of Atonement. In that typical service the sanctuary was cleansed with the blood of animal sacrifices but the heavenly things are purified with the perfect sacrifice of the blood of Jesus. The investigative judgment reveals to heavenly intelligences that among the dead are asleep in Christ and therefore, in Him, are deemed worthy to have part in the first resurrection. It also makes manifest who among the living are abiding in Christ, keeping the commandments of God and the faith of Jesus, and in Him, therefore, are ready for translation into His everlasting kingdom. This judgment vindicates the justice of God in saving those who believe in Jesus. It declares that those who have remained loyal to God shall receive the kingdom. The completion of this ministry of Christ will mark the close of human probation before the Second Advent. (Hebrews 8:1-5; 4:14-16; 9:11-28; 10:19-22; 1:3; 2:16, 17; Daniel 7:9-27; 8:13, 14; 9:24-27; Numbers 14:34; Ezekiel 4:6; Leviticus 16; Revelation 14:6, 7; 20:12; 14:12; 22:12.)

25. Second Coming of Christ:

The second coming of Christ is the blessed hope of the church, the grand climax of the gospel. The Savior's coming will be literal, personal, visible, and worldwide. When He returns, the righteous dead will be resurrected, and together with the righteous living will be glorified and taken to heaven, but the unrighteous will die. The almost complete fulfillment of most lines of prophecy, together with the present condition of the world, indicates that Christ's coming is imminent. The time of that event has not been revealed, and we are therefore exhorted to be ready at all times. (Titus 2:13; Hebrews 9:28; John 14:1-3; Acts 1:9-11; Matthew 24:14; Revelation 1:7; Matthew 24:43, 44; 1 Thessalonians 4:13-18; 1 Corinthians 15:51-54, 2 Thessalonians 1:7-10; 2:8, Revelation 14:14-20; 19:11-21; Matthew 21; Mark 13; Luke 21:2, 2 Timothy 3:1-5, 1 Thessalonians 5:1-6.)

26. Death and Resurrection:

The wages of sin is death. But God, who alone is immortal, will grant eternal life to His redeemed. Until that day death is an unconscious state for all people. When Christ, who is our life, appears, the resurrected righteous and the living righteous will be glorified and caught up to meet their Lord. The second resurrection, the resurrection of the unrighteous, will take place a thousand years later. (Romans 6:23; 1 Timothy 6:15, 16; Ecclesiastes 9:5, 6; Psalms 146:3, 4; John 11:11-14; Colossians 3:4; 1 Corinthians 15:51-54; 1 Thessalonians 4:13-17; John 5:28, 29; Revelation 20:1-10.)

27. Millennium and the End of Sin:

The millennium is the thousand-year reign of Christ with His saints in heaven between the first and second resurrections. During this time the wicked dead will be judged; the earth will be utterly desolate, without living human inhabitants, but occupied by Satan and his angels. At its close Christ with His saints and the Holy City will descend from heaven to earth. The unrighteous dead will then be resurrected, and with Satan and his angels will surround the city; but fire from God will consume them and cleanse the earth. The universe will thus be freed of sin and sinners forever. (Revelation 20; 1 Corinthians 6:2, 3; Jeremiah 4:23-26; Revelation 21:1-5; Malachi 4:1; Ezekiel 28:18, 19.)

28. New Earth:

On the new earth, in which righteousness dwells, God will provide an eternal home for the redeemed and a perfect environment for everlasting life, love, joy, and learning in His presence. For here God Himself will dwell with His people, and suffering and death will have passed away. The great controversy will be ended, and sin will be no more. All things, animate and inanimate, will declare that God is love; and He shall reign forever. Amen. (2 Peter 3:13; Isaiah 35; 65:17-25; Matthew 5:5; Revelation 21:1-7; 22:15; 11:15.)

Significantly, belief in the Sabbath, the seventh-day of the week, and in the advent, sets Adventists apart from the rest of the Christian world. Adventists are therefore those who *believe* and *worship* on the seventh-day Sabbath and look forward to the *advent* (the second coming of Christ.)

The Seventh-day Adventist Church had its roots in the Millerite movement of the 1830s and 1840s, during the period of the Second Great Awakening, in United States of America. During the time, as a result of misinterpretation of the scriptures, Miller and his fellow Bible students believed that Jesus would return in 1843. When the time they believed Jesus would return came and passed, they went back to the scriptures and discovered an error in their calculation. As a result of their new calculation, they set the advent to be in 1844. They were disappointed once again as Jesus, as we all know, didn't show up. The disappointment was so great and so bitter that some of the believers abandoned the movement and went back to their former churches. The Millerite emphasis in searching the Bible was to get proper interpretation of the prophecies about the end of time in the Books of Daniel and Revelation.

Then I heard a holy one speaking, and another holy one said to him, "How long will it take for the vision to be fulfilled—the vision concerning the daily sacrifice, the rebellion that causes desolation, and the surrender of the sanctuary and the host that would be trampled underfoot?" He said to me, "It will take 2300 evenings and mornings; then the sanctuary will be reconsecrated." Daniel 8:13-14 (NIV)

Given the prophetic time of one day for one year in Ezekiel 4:5 and 6, the Millerites believed that the decree of the King of Persia, found in Ezra 7, which was given in 457 BC, would end in 1843. When this failed they thought it would end in 1844. They did not take into account what Peter said in 2 Peter 3:10: *But the day of the Lord will come like a thief. The heavens will disappear with a roar; the elements will be destroyed by fire, and the earth and everything in it will be laid bare.* (NIV)

Or what Jesus said to His disciples in Mark 13:32-37:

V32 *"But of that day and hour no one knows, not even the angels in heaven, nor the Son, but only the Father.* V33 *Take heed, watch and pray; for you do not know when the time is."* V34 *It is like a man going to a far country, who left his house and gave authority to his servants and to each his work, and commanded the doorkeeper to watch.* V35 *Watch therefore, for you do not know when the master of the house is coming—in the evening, at midnight, at the crowing of the rooster, or in the morning.* V36 *lest, coming suddenly, he find you sleeping.* V37 *And what I say to you, I say to all: Watch!* (NKJV)

Triumph Through Faith

Even after the disappointments of 1843 and 1844, the scriptures were carefully searched, with earnest thought and prayer and after a period of suspense, light shone and doubt and uncertainty were swept away. Here is E. G. White's description of the events:

Instead of the prophecy of Daniel 8:14 referring to the purifying of the earth, it was now plain that it pointed to the closing of work of our High Priest in Heaven, the finishing of the atonement, and the preparing of the people to abide the day of his coming. (Life Sketches of Ellen G. White, Page 63)

They learned the truth when they earnestly searched the scriptures. Even today, there may be something in the Bible that God may not have revealed. Christians, historians, philosophers and all serious scholars should earnestly search the scriptures with prayer, and one day God will reveal another secret to His people through them. Since acquisition of knowledge is regenerative, those who aspire to acquire spiritual and scriptural knowledge are encouraged to work hard. Who knows, another scriptural milestone may be realized, like it happened to Ellen G. White and the Millerites. The Seventh-day Adventists owe its establishment and existence to them.

From the General Conference of Seventh-day Adventist records, we know that the Adventist Church was founded in 1863, in New England, in the United States of America. Prominent figures in the early church included Hiram Edson, James Springer White and his wife Ellen G. White, Joseph Bates and J. N. Andrews.

Over the coming decades the church expanded from its original base in New England to become an international movement. Significant developments of the twentieth

Arrival of Seventh-day Adventism in Kenya

century led to its recognition as a Christian denomination.

In 1860, the fledgling movement finally settled on the name Seventh-day Adventist, representative of the church's distinguishing beliefs. Three years later, on May 21, 1863, the General Conference of Seventh-day Adventist was formed and the movement became an official organization.

The first regional annual camp meeting took place in 1868, September. Since then, the annual camp meeting has become a pattern among the Seventh-day Adventists worldwide and is still practiced today.

The President of the General Conference is the head of the General Conference of Seventh-day Adventists—the governing body of the Seventh-day Adventist Church.

The President's office is within the offices of the General Conference, located in Silver Spring, Maryland, United States of America. Traditionally, an American has held the post.

Of the seventeen presidents, thirteen were born in the United States, one in Puerto Rico to North American Missionaries; one in Australia and two in Norway, of which one emigrated to the US at age five.

12

VISION

The measure of life, after all, is not its duration but its donation.
(Corrie ten Boom)

I am alive to the possibility that someone will entirely miss the reason for including church statistics and institutions in this book. I have not done so to attribute such extraordinary successes that have been achieved by the church to Pastor Silfano. Mine has only been to highlight the foresight and vision that led the humble pastor to see the bigger picture and act to bring his people into the fold of the remnant church.

Pastor Silfano later lived to a ripe old age, and old age is knowledge, experience; it is success and prosperity to those who allow the Lord to live in them—in righteousness. But the devil does not allow such people to live in peace. They go through tribulation and turbulence in life and endure cruel temptations. They sometimes look miserable because they are seen to suffer more than their peers, who don't know God. But inwardly, they are a happier lot, for there is happiness in having Jesus

Vision

as a personal savior. Joseph overcame Satan's temptations; Job overcame grueling temptations and won a ferocious battle; and Daniel overcame Satan's intrigues. We can all win if we cling to the Lord and allow Him into our hearts.

Pastor Silfano clung to the Lord and allowed Him to guide and guard him every step of his earthly life, all the while preparing his peaceful exit. He prepared his children well for that day. He prepared his church family, his village and his friends for that day. He prepared his peers and some of them who were smart took a cue and prepared their people too, both for the final exit and the inevitable transition. A cousin of mine took a cue and wrote his own eulogy while still alive. In it he talked about himself (life history) and even decided who would read it. He also named the pastor to preside over his funeral. My uncle (Nicodemo) directed that I be the only one to eulogize him at his funeral. Some have designated churches other than the ones they fellowship in to preside at their funerals. Some took care of the distribution of their wealth to their loved ones while still alive, but in anticipation of their exit. Some have even directed the way their body should be disposed of either through burial or through cremation. The pastor made it easy for his people to contemplate death and act to make the burden light on those left behind.

Through premonition, Pastor Silfano knew he would exit soon and made necessary preparations. He talked to his family, preparing them for the fateful day, instructing them what to do when the day came. He talked to his in-laws and the parents of his sons- and daughters-in-law. He had a long conversation with me over what he wished our people to be, the vision he had for them—his children and grandchildren. This was the last time he talked with me before he passed away.

He had good dreams for his family. He wanted them to continue being honest, respectful and passionate. He stressed that with these attributes his family would surmount obstacles and prosper. He expected them to have confidence and belief in themselves. One must believe in himself to be able to have the kind of confidence that will propel him or her to greater prosperity, he said. He needed them to be foresighted by taking care of their families and property zealously. He needed them to aspire to acquire knowledge at all cost. On this he didn't give them options, because in knowledge there is greatness and in greatness there is honour and respect, which is what everybody wants.

He wanted them to be industrious, without which he knew they would be beggars. He confided in me that he had implored them to work hard in all their endeavors. When I talked to his eldest son, Pastor Tobias Otieno Ayayo, later, he confirmed that his daddy couldn't complete a session of counseling or pep talk without stressing the importance of hard work. It was his wish that his family and descendants remain in the Adventist faith, as Jesus, through the church, would be their shield and protector from the devil and his temptations.

Pastor Silfano told me that the greatest legacy he was bequeathing his family and his people was his faith, his church and his Christ. They had to babysit, cultivate and nurture this bequest for prosperity to blossom in their midst. Those who embraced this vision struck it rich and are blessed, but those who didn't weren't so lucky—the difference between them is glaring.

He fought so hard for his people because he envisioned a time when they would be a people like everybody else. He dreamed that they would one day take life more seriously by stopping quail-keeping, excessive use of alcohol and smoking of bhang. He wished them to crave for book knowledge, and also spiritual knowledge. Whereas he could not get everyone to convert to

Vision

Adventism, he wished his people to have a flag post and a post office box number, where each could stand and be counted. Whatever faith one believed in, one had to cling to it and serve it diligently. For the Adventists, it was his wish that evangelism should take center stage in their lives. He dreamed of a period when there would be a proliferation of Adventist churches in our area. This has since come to pass because we today have at least a church in a radius of one kilometer. The planting of churches has been a success beyond our wildest imagination. Other churches have not been left behind. Evangelical churches, like New Apostolic and Church of Christ in Africa, are doing equally well.

Pastor Silfano had one stern warning for his Adventist adherents—never backslide! He wanted his people to embrace the culture of hard work, to till their farms, engage in viable businesses and be industrious in whatever task they took upon themselves to do. Rather than busying themselves with drinking and playing *ajwa* (an African game played by two people from a plank of timber on which 16 holes are drilled, eight on each side and dried fruits of *ngeta,* which is an African plant producing the fruits, the kernels of which are used in playing this game. These kernels must be twenty four). He desired that his people should eat in order to live, not live in order to eat.

On political leadership, having been a bone of contention in the past, he dreamed that one day his people would make it to Parliament. There have been serious attempts at achieving this by the writer in Gem Constituency, Sam Okello in Muhoroni Constituency, and Cleveland Otieno Ayayo, his grandson, Uriri Constituency. There have also been several councillors and chairpersons of County Councils and a mayor.

He had a vision that the people would continue to provide leadership in the civil service of the Government of Kenya as he had broken the barrier that prevented them from reaching that level. His people have since produced permanent secretaries, a judge, state counsel, a district commissioner and district officers, directors in various ministries, accountants, chiefs and assistant chiefs. His people no longer beg for these positions, they compete for them because they have the necessary qualifications, and get them on merit.

After this fruitful conversation, which took place in my Milimani home, in Kisumu, he prayed for me like never before. As one of his favorite nephews, he had a soft spot for me and wanted to bless me. Through his prayers, I believe he blessed me abundantly. Because of him, I am what I am.

***

Like many elders his age, Pastor Silfano suffered from some of the ailments of his peers: high blood pressure, prostate complications, a failing heart and diabetes, but it was hypertension and diabetes that caused him a lot of discomfort. He had to watch what he ate at all times. He avoided foods with too much sugar, glucose or cholesterol. He was also concerned about the cleanliness of the food and cleanliness of the environment it was prepared in. He was equally conscious about the cleanliness of his hands. To this end he insisted on using fork, knife and spoon when eating. This also helped him regulate the quantity of food he ingested.

He visited several health facilities for treatment, but did not pull through; he eventually succumbed to his illness on the 21st day of April 1984. He was seventy-seven.

He was survived by his widow by second marriage Esther Achieng Ayayo, his sons Tobias Otieno, ABC Ocholla, Amos Ochieng, Samuel Ayieko, Jacob Okoth, Thadayo Mijema,

Vision

Moses Oswago, Jeremiah Ochieng, Elijah Opondo and Jonathan Ogweno; his daughters Beldina Akeyo, Joice Akumu, Loice Anyango, and Asenath Awuor; his grandchildren Edwina Atieno Ombado, Martin Omondi, Stephen Ochieng, Dr Zachary Ngalo, Paul Oluoch, Cleveland Okoth, Christine Adhiambo, Rena Alberta, James Ayodo, Jenny Ocholla, Margaritta Akinyi, Erick Ochola, Asenath Ngalo Wamalwa, Dorcus Awino, Alice Adikinyi, Millicent Akoth, Beryl Adhiambo, Kenneth Kaunda (Ochieng), Eastings Odhiambo, Pamela Akoth (Ngolo), Mabel Awino, Asenath Achieng, Jackline Odhiambo, Erick Odhiambo, Duncan Odipo, Edwin Oluoch, Jane Aduke (Awuor), Mary Akinyi, David Otieno, Alice Atieno, Asenath Ngalo, Linet Ndira, Joseph Onyango, Roseline Awino, Beatrice Atieno Nyangulu. He also left behind a number of great grandchildren.

***

Through faith Pastor Silfano won the struggle for emancipation of his people. Through faith he established a school for his people and employed teachers to teach therein. Through faith he shuttered the barrier, which for a long time, stood in the way of his people and administrative leadership. More significantly, he, through faith, brought the Seventh-day Adventist Church to his people, which was later used as a vehicle to attain education, prosperity, and spiritual righteousness. Without the church our people would still have been languishing in abject poverty and backwardness.

Like Moses to the Israelites, no leader has risen among our people like Pastor Silfano. Leaders come and go, but none has attained the level of perfection, courage, vision and righteousness like Pastor Silfano. Like Moses, he led his people out of bondage and God helped him along the way.

Triumph Through Faith

In Deuteronomy 34:10-12, the writer underscores the might of Moses thus:

Since then, no prophet has risen in Israel like Moses, whom the LORD knew face-to-face, who did all those miraculous signs and wonders the LORD sent him to do in Egypt—to Pharaoh and all his officials and to his whole land. For no one has ever shown the mighty power or performed the awesome deeds that Moses did in the sight of all Israel. (NIV)

Pastor Silfano Ayayo (in suit) greeting Jaramogi Oginga Odinga at the victory party of the writer in 1980. Looking on are Mzee Wasonga Sijeyo (left) and the writer.

Pastor Silfano Ayayo praying at the victory party of the writer. Also in the picture are (from left to right): Michael Olendo Meso, Wasonga Sijeyo, O. M. T. Adala and the writer.

13

RETIREMENT

You find the meaning in life by giving yourself away not by satisfying yourself. The most gratifying thing, at Seventy-three years old, is to be able to think that your life was used to help others. (Chuck Colson)

Ever since God rested on the seventh day, upon completion of the six days of creation work, man has had the obligation to rest once every week, in addition to the nightly rest. The working class has an annual leave added to those rests. These rests are essential to workers to enable them to give optimum output. Those who do physical work need to give their exhausted bodies a rest, while those using mental power need to give their brains a rest too. We need rest as we tackle our chores. None other than God himself set the example in Genesis 2:2-3. It says:

And on the seventh day, God ended His work which He had done, and he rested on the seventh day from all his work which He had done. Then God blessed the seventh day and sanctified it, because in it He rested from His work which God had created and made. (NKJV)

By this rest God set a weekly cycle of seven days, which has withstood the test of time. He also set a day cycle, beginning with sunset and ending on the following sunset. In Genesis 1:5, it says:

God called the light Day and the darkness He called Night. So the evening and the morning were the first day. (NKJV)

God's day cycle begins at sundown and ends the following sundown. Although the period between one sunset and the next varies from place to place, depending on the geographical position of that place on the earth's surface, and the earth's position in relation to the sun, God, in His infinite wisdom, used sunset to sunset as the standard measure of time for one day. The point is, *there is nowhere on planet earth where there is no sunrise and sunset.* Through God, mankind has been able to work out a universally acceptable measure of time. Through Him, mankind has daily and weekly rest periods, and even an annual rest period. Whereas there is no dispute on the day cycle man is supposed to rest, the weekly rest has generated a lot of controversy, with some insisting it is on Sunday—the first day of the week. Others think it is Friday—the sixth day of the week. Others even say it can be any day of the week!

Matthew, writing in chapter 28:1, was categorical that Sunday was the first day of the week. Listen to him speak:

After the Sabbath, at dawn on the first day of the week. (NIV)

Later Mark, writing in chapter 16:2, captured this vividly. He said:

Very early on the first day of the week, just after sunrise they were on their way to the tomb. (NIV)

Retirement

Do you get it? The scripture (the Bible) is explicit that "the rest day is the seventh day of the week, which is the Sabbath, the origin of which is anchored on Genesis 2:3. This verse says:

And God blessed the seventh day and made it holy, because on it He rested from all the work of creating that He had done. (NIV)

It is clear. The seventh day rest has been observed since creation. The Israelites, in their exodus under Moses, observed it. The description is in Exodus 16:23. And this is probably one of the most graphic descriptions of Sabbath observance by a people in the Bible. Let's take a look:

He said to them, "This is what the LORD commanded: Tomorrow is to be a day of rest, a holy Sabbath to the LORD. So bake what you want to bake and boil what you want to boil. Save whatever is left and keep it until morning." So they saved it until morning, as Moses commanded, and it did not stink or get maggots in it. "Eat it today," Moses said, because today is a Sabbath to the LORD. You will not find any of it on the ground today. Six days you are to gather it, but on the Seventh day, the Sabbath, there will not be any."

The Sabbath was mandated and hallowed by God. In Exodus 20:8 and 11, we find the most direct command of the Lord regarding Sabbath rest. The Lord says: *Remember the Sabbath day by keeping it holy.*

And earlier, Isaiah, one of the greatest prophets ever, captures the joy Sabbath-keepers have in his writings. He says, in Isaiah 58:13, thus:

If you keep your feet from breaking the Sabbath and from doing as you please on my holy day, if you call the Sabbath a delight and the LORD's holy day honourable, and if you honor it by not going your own way and not doing as you please or speaking idle words, then you will find your joy in the LORD. (NIV)

When Christ came along, He built a ring around the Sabbath by keeping the day holy. This He did even though He was also LORD of the Sabbath.

Then Jesus said to them, "The Son of Man is Lord of the Sabbath." Luke 6:5 (NIV)

But what is the full meaning of this Sabbath, which we are commanded by God to observe and keep holy? In one of the letters to the Hebrews, by an unknown author, the full meaning of Sabbath is stated. We find it in Hebrews 4:8-11, where it says:

For if Joshua had given them rest, God would not have spoken later about another day. There remains, then, a Sabbath rest for the people of God; for anyone who enters God's rest also rests from his own work, just as God did from His. Let us, therefore, make every effort to enter that rest, so that no one will fall by following their example of disobedience. (NIV)

Unlike other species, which have only two rests, human species have four rests in their lifespan. They have:

Nightly rest – sleeping

Weekly rest – Sabbath-keeping

Rest after leaving office or employment because of age – retirement

Final rest – death

Pastor Silfano had so far had the first two forms of rest. Now the time had come to experience the third and the final.

But let me begin from the beginning.

He had started his evangelization work with the Seventh-day Adventist Church at thirty-seven. Although the colonial government had set the retirement age for Kenyan workers at fifty-five, which was later adopted by the native government,

Retirement

the clergy, particularly the Adventist ones, could stay in the ministry as long as they could walk and read the Bible. This was because there was a serious shortage of evangelists because few had been trained.

Pastor Silfano did not wait to be infirm to opt out of service. He retired in 1965 at the age of fifty-eight.

Retirement age has since been raised to sixty due to improved life expectancy, and to reward experience and give employees a lifeline to enable them to see their children through education. Pastor Silfano retired when he was still strong in body and mind, thanks to the way he was brought up and the African diet of the day. Most African families of the day, from my tribe, lived on Daniel's diet, a healthy, balanced diet consisting mainly of milk products and vegetables. Some people considered this poor man's diet, but it ensured longevity and less health complications. The pastor retired to have time in his twilight years with his family, and to reflect on his achievements. He retired a happy man and never changed much in his disposition and demeanor during retirement. He remained the live wire he was before—a respectable church member of his village church and a revered member of the village community. To his wife he was a partner, a provider and a comforter. To his children, old and young, he was a fountain of knowledge and a polished storyteller.

His magnanimity continued unabated, and he extended this, not only to his immediate family, but also to his extended family and everybody else. He was as good in retirement as he was during his working life. He continued to keep livestock and poultry and had time to improve the face of his home. He doubled his farming activities and reaped handsomely.

Although he got many children in old age, through his second marriage, God provided for them and ensured they had food on the table, went to school and dressed well. No wonder they stuck to the church and some of them became church elders and evangelists. They did well because of their faith in God. God blessed them abundantly too.

He took advantage of this opportunity in his life to visit relatives and the parents of his daughters-in-law. He made occasional visits to his brothers, cousins, and brothers-in-law, in Gem. Every time he went to Gem, he passed through this writer's home in Kisumu and shared with him his experiences. It was from these visits that the writer got much of the information used in this book. His relationship with his brothers, cousins and in-laws was cordial.

And so retired the servant of God and of the people!